Slaveiko Gospodinov

Algorithmic logic

Slaveiko Gospodinov

# Algorithmic logic

ScienciaScripts

**Imprint**

Any brand names and product names mentioned in this book are subject to trademark, brand or patent protection and are trademarks or registered trademarks of their respective holders. The use of brand names, product names, common names, trade names, product descriptions etc. even without a particular marking in this work is in no way to be construed to mean that such names may be regarded as unrestricted in respect of trademark and brand protection legislation and could thus be used by anyone.

Cover image: www.ingimage.com

This book is a translation from the original published under ISBN 978-620-6-84640-6.

Publisher:
Sciencia Scripts
is a trademark of
Dodo Books Indian Ocean Ltd. and OmniScriptum S.R.L publishing group

120 High Road, East Finchley, London, N2 9ED, United Kingdom
Str. Armeneasca 28/1, office 1, Chisinau MD-2012, Republic of Moldova, Europe
Printed at: see last page
ISBN: 978-620-8-27833-5

# Contents

## Introduction

Every theory has basic concepts, which are related to each other, are in certain terminological relations [1] and form a coherent semantic network. The semantic network can be considered as a discrete information field [2-12] or a terminological field [13]. A concept has a denotation and a scope [14-17]. While the denotation is usually stable, the content tends to change or to polysemy. New connections, interpretations and interpretations emerge for an initially emerged concept. This happens because of the diversity of processes of the surrounding world. The basis for studying the world around us is the information field. It contains generalised information about various objects like a photograph. When studying the information field, new regularities are revealed [18]. New regularities make changes in the existing system of concepts and relations between them. They can either change the definition or the scope of a concept. The object of study of this monograph is the concepts of "logic" and "algorithm". The concepts of logic and algorithm are interpreted in an extended way. . The term "algorithm", as well as the term "information" [19-24] has undergone significant changes in interpretation and attribution to different categories. In the process of development, terms are subject to derivation [25-27] and term formation. An example is the term "algorithmicisation" [28-30], which refers to the many processes of constructing an algorithm. To date, there are many ways and principles of algorithmicisation. Different ways are applied depending on the accumulated experience, the condition of the task at hand and the availability of resources for its solution. One of the principles of algorithmisation is the logical construction of an algorithm [31-34] or logical algorithmisation. Logical algorithmicisation is a procedure of algorithm construction based on logical principles. Logical algorithmicisation is the first step not only in the construction of algorithms, but also in the construction of complex systems, in system analysis [35-42] and functional analysis [43-47]. Algorithm construction often occurs as a process of logical inference or decision making. The modern stage of development of sciences is characterised by the presence of interdisciplinarity and increasing complexity of information processing. These factors are also reflected in the development of algorithmisation. Nowadays there are different types of algorithms and methods of their construction. Logical algorithmicisation is the basic principle.

One of the important principles of algorithm construction and logical algorithmicisation is the correspondence principle. In a simple version, it is the principle of information correspondence [48-50]. It exists in information processes [51, 52] and in modelling [53]. In essence, it is a procedural information correspondence. It should be noted that the concept of correspondence is interpreted differently. In one case it is considered as a relation [48-50], in another case as a process. E.K. Voishvilo [54] gives such a definition of procedural correspondence: "The principle of correspondence is the law of knowledge development". He considers correspondence as a process of development between the old and the new. In this case, it can be interpreted as a connection. Voishvilo [54] points out the relation of "successive theories". ". It refers to cases when instead of one theory relating to some area of reality, a new one appears, possibly with a wider area, but including the area of the former theory. At the same time, this new theory gives a more accurate understanding of some relations of the old theory" Another situation of inconsistency is possible, when the new theory rejects the old theory. For example, the heliocentric picture of the world has replaced the geocentric picture. Logic also, as well as algorithm has significantly expanded its interpretation [55-80].

## 1. peculiarities of algorithmic logic

The term "algorithmic logic" is used in a narrow and a broad sense. In the narrow sense [81], algorithmic logic (AL1) combines logical techniques that are used to construct and verify algorithms. It is also interpreted as programming logic. AL1 is an essential tool for every computer scientist.

In a broad sense [64, 65], algorithmic logic (AL2) includes algorithmic techniques for logical constructions, reasoning and analyses. For example, from these positions, the system of syllogisms belongs to algorithmic logic. A system of any inference constructs that has a repeating pattern can be referred to algorithmic logic.

Algorithmic logic (AL 1) provides a set of logical axioms and inference rules suitable for analysing the properties and capabilities of algorithms. It serves as a tool for formalisation and verification of algorithms. It serves as a logical justification of algorithms. Algorithmic properties are expressed by logical formulas. Therefore, the analysis of algorithms, i.e. their verification and efficiency evaluation, can be based on algorithmic logic. However, logical formulas alone are not enough to construct an algorithm. Algorithm construction is completed with the help of functionalological constructions. The same programme can have many interpretations. Unambiguous interpretation of interpretation due to syntactic rules. Syntax determines which expressions are correctly (or logically) formed. But it does not determine the meaning of an expression. Therefore, syntax complements functionally logical constructions and computations. The process of computation can also be subject to logical analysis. All this together determines the logical reasoning of calculations. It includes four components: logical constructions, functional-logical constructions, syntax of constructions, logical correctness of calculations.

For computations that are sequences of states, the most important question is whether the computation is finite or infinite. This question is solved by logical reasoning and leads to AL2. Qualitative [82-85] and comparative [86-89] analyses are also based on AL2.

AL2 is a necessary foundation for a researcher in the field of cognition. This foundation serves as the basis for knowledge acquisition [90-94] in the field of computer science [95, 96]. Meanwhile, algorithms and logical techniques are also used directly for knowledge acquisition [97, 98].

This foundation serves as the basis for spatial knowledge acquisition [99, 100] in the field of geoinformatics [101]. AL2 serves as a foundation for identifying implicit knowledge [102-104] and transforming it into explicit knowledge [105, 106]. AL2 requires the construction of a reasoning system for different cases.

Before trying to construct a system of reasoning about properties of programmes or objects, one should find a way to express them in the form of formulas. The basis of such an expression is a formal language. In computer science it is an information language [107]. In a particular case it is the language of information units [108-110].

## 1.1 Argumentation and logic

Argumentation is a part of algorithmic logic. The theory of argumentation has its origins in fundamentalism, theory of knowledge (epistemology) and in the field of philosophy. It sought to find the grounds for claims in argumentative forms, in materials (factual laws), and in a universal system of knowledge. The dialectical method was made famous by Plato. It was used by Socrates, critically questioning the actions of historical figures. Scientists- gradually rejected the systematic philosophy of Aristotle and the idealism of Plato and Kant. They rejected the idea that the premises of argumentation derive their validity from formal philosophical systems.

Argumentation theory is an interdisciplinary scientific field. Argumentation theory explores not only the processes of inference but also the processes of persuasion and refutation. It includes the skills of debate, dialogue, conversation and persuasion. It studies inference rules, logic and procedural rules in both artificial and real-world settings [111].

Argumentation involves discussion and negotiation related to joint decision-making procedures [112]. Speaking the language of informatics, argumentation includes information gathering, information interaction [113] and information influence [114]. The technology of argumentation includes communications: eristic dialogue; social debate, in which defeating the opponent is the main goal; didactic dialogue used for teaching [115] Argumentation is an art and a science. They are often the means by which people defend their beliefs or personal interests. Through argumentation, people either decide to change personal beliefs or not.

Argumentation is widely used in law, for example, in court proceedings, in preparing arguments and in testing the validity of evidence. In addition, argumentation is used in a posteriori rationalisations, by which actors try to justify decisions that they have made irrationally.

Argumentation in the process of communication is sometimes interpreted as discourse. It is one of the four rhetorical forms, along with exposition, description and narration. The study of argumentation, its technology and its problems is of great importance, first of all, for artificial intelligence systems.

Decision making in technical fields and psychology. For a comparative analysis of reasoning and logic [116], a comparison can be made with decision making in technical sciences and in psychology. In technical sciences, decision making is deterministic, formalised and logical. It can be depicted by a diagram in the form of a logical chain or a procedural chain that corresponds to a logical chain. In technical sciences, decision making is often depicted in the form of an algorithm. Decision-making is seen as a technological process independent of the subject. In technical sciences, decision making is an objective or objectivised process. In technical sciences, decision-making is based on system analysis and logic.

In psychology, decision-making is viewed as a cognitive process involving subject A and subject or object B. It is a process that leads to the selection of a belief or course of action among several possible alternatives. The choice can be rational or irrational. Decision making is a reasoning process based on assumptions, about contingent values, about the preferences and beliefs of the decision maker. Every decision-making process leads to choices that may or may not prompt action. In psychology, decision making is based on qualitative, comparative and cognitive analysis with elements of system analysis and logical analysis. In psychology, decision-making is a subjective process.

Factors of Argumentation. To analyse the essence of argumentation it is necessary to consider its key positions.

Argumentation is preceded by understanding and identifying the arguments, explicit or implicit, and the goals of the participants in different types of dialogue. Argumentation is preceded by identifying and analysing the premises from which conclusions are drawn.

Preceding the argumentation is the establishment of the "burden of proof" [117], that is, identifying the subject and his or her arguments about the original statement and his or her responsibility to provide evidence, and justifying why that position deserves to be accepted.

For the principal or attorney who bears the "burden of proof," it is necessary to gather evidence for his or her position in order to persuade or compel the opponent to agree. The method by which this is achieved is by making sound, sensible and convincing arguments that are devoid of weaknesses and not subject to criticism.

In the "burden of proof" debate." [117] creates a "burden of objection" [117]. It is necessary to identify fallacies in the opponent's argumentation, attack their causes, and provide counterexamples. Within the "burden of proof" one must identify fallacies of the "burden of objection". It is necessary to show why the correct conclusion cannot be derived from the reasons given for its argumentation from the "burden of objections".

Preferably, classical logic should be used as a method of reasoning, so that the conclusion logically follows from the assumptions [118]. One of the problems with logical reasoning is that if a set of assumptions is inconsistent, anything can logically follow from the inconsistency. It is therefore common practice to insist that the set of assumptions be consistent. It is also good practice to insist that the set of assumptions be the minimum set, relative to the inclusion of the set, necessary to derive a consequence. Such arguments are called MINCON arguments, short for minimally consistent. Such reasoning is used in the fields of law and medicine.

Argumentation Methodology. An argument usually has an internal structure with three main components.

A set of assumptions or presuppositions.

Method of reasoning or argumentation

Conclusion, conclusion, or point of view.

An argument has one or more premises and one conclusion. In a common form, an argument involves two or more communicators. One communicator 1 argues for a point of view, another communicator2 or opponent argues for a different position. Both communicators try to persuade each other. Different types of dialogue [119] or informational communication are used.

• Persuasion dialogue aims to resolve conflicting viewpoints of different positions.

• Negotiations aim to resolve conflicts of interest through co-operation and bargaining.

• Awareness is aimed at eliminating general ignorance by increasing knowledge.

• Deliberation aims to fulfil the need for action by making a decision.

• Eristics seeks to resolve a situation of antagonism through verbal combat.

Dialogue or communication is preceded by a search for information, which aims to reduce the ignorance of one party [120]. Nowadays, the term "argumentation" is closely related to the concept of "communication". As a consequence, the concept of "argumentation communication" has emerged. Communication is a broader technology compared to logic.

Logical reasoning is directed in one direction from communicator 1 to communicator 2. It is rigid and not adaptive. In the presence of contradictions, it is fallacious and leads to errors. Argumentative communication is two-way and adaptive. It includes communicators in the argumentation system and is flexible and adaptive.

Nowadays different types of argumentation are distinguished: conversational, mathematical, scientific, interpretive, legal, judicial, logical, political, communicative, cognitive.

Conversational argumentation has become a recognised force in sociology, anthropology, linguistics, speech communication and psychology [120]. Some scholars (e.g., Ralph X. Johnson) interpret the term "argument" narrowly, as exclusively written discourse or even discourse in which all premises are explicit. Others (e.g., Michael Gilbert) interpret the term "argument" broadly to include oral and even non-verbal discourse, such as the extent to which a war memorial or propaganda poster can argue or "make an argument." The philosopher S. Toulmin has said that an argument is a claim on our attention and our belief, a point of view that would seem to authorise the consideration of, say, propaganda posters as arguments. The argument between broad and narrow theorists has been going on for a long time and is unlikely to be resolved. The views of most argumentation theorists and analysts fall somewhere between these two extremes.

Mathematical argumentation is related to the philosophy of mathematics and the search for mathematical truth. The concept of argument has long existed in mathematics, but in a slightly different sense than in logic and argumentation. If an argument can be represented as propositions of symbolic logic, then it can be verified by applying generally accepted proof procedures. This has been done for arithmetic using Peano's axioms. An argument in mathematics considers an argument valid only if it can be shown that it cannot have true premises and a false conclusion.

Scientific argumentation is linked to the social foundations of scientific knowledge in Alan G. Gross's book The *Rhetoric of Science* (Cambridge: Harvard University Press, 1990) [121]. Gross believes that science is rhetorical "without remainder", meaning that scientific knowledge itself cannot be seen as an idealised basis of knowledge. Scientific knowledge is produced rhetorically, which means that it has a special epistemological authority only insofar as its general methods of verification are credible. Such thinking represents an almost complete rejection of the foundationalism on which argumentation was originally based.

Interpretive argumentation is a dialogical process in which participants explore and/or resolve interpretations, often of a text of any medium that contains significant ambiguity in meaning. Interpretive argumentation is relevant to the humanities, hermeneutics, literary theory, linguistics, semantics, pragmatics, semiotics, analytic philosophy, and aesthetics. Conceptual interpretation topics include aesthetic, legal, logical, and religious interpretation. Topics in scientific interpretation include scientific modelling

Psychology has long studied the non-logical aspects of argumentation. For example, research has shown that simply repeating an idea is often a more effective method of argumentation than appealing to reason. Propaganda often uses repetition. [122] "Repeat a lie often enough and it will become true" is a law of propaganda often attributed to Nazi politician Joseph Goebbels. Nazi rhetoric has been widely studied as a campaign of repetition, among other things. Empirical studies of a communicator's authority and attractiveness, sometimes referred to as charisma, have also been closely related to empirical argumentation. Such studies bring argumentation into the framework of persuasion theory and practice.

Some psychologists, such as William J. McGuire, believe that the syllogism is the basic unit of human thinking. They have produced a great deal of empirical work on McGuire's famous title "A Syllogistic Analysis of Cognitive Relationships". The central line of this way of thinking is that logic is contaminated by psychological variables such as "wishful thinking" in which subjects confuse the probability of predictions with the desirability of predictions. People hear what they want to hear and see what they expect to see. If planners want something to happen, they believe it should happen. If they hope something doesn't happen, they believe it is unlikely to happen. Thus, smokers think they will personally avoid cancer, promiscuous sexual activity practises unsafe sex

Field of Arguments. In consonance with the information field theory [123], the argument field theory has been put forward in argumentation theory. Stephen Toulmin and Charles Arthur Willard have argued for the idea of argument fields, the former drawing on Ludwig Wittgenstein's notion of language games (Sprachspiel), the latter drawing on communication and argumentation theory, sociology, political science and social epistemology. For Toulmin, the term 'field' denotes the discourses in which arguments and factual claims are grounded (124). For Willard, the term "field" is interchangeable with "community," "audience," or "readership." [125] Similarly, J. Thomas Goodnight studied "fields". arguments and generated a large literature by younger scholars responding to or utilising his ideas [126]. The general sense of these field theories is that the premises of arguments derive their meaning from social communities [127].

In many of his writings, Toulmin has pointed out that absolutism (represented by theoretical or analytical arguments) has limited practical value. Absolutism derives from Plato's idealised formal logic, which defends universal truth; accordingly, absolutists believe that moral problems can be solved by adhering to a standard set of moral principles, regardless of context.

On the contrary, Toulmin argues that many of these so-called standard principles are irrelevant to real-life situations that people encounter in everyday life.

To develop his claim, Toulmin introduced the notion of argument fields. In "The Use of Argument" (1958) [124], Toulmin argues that some aspects of arguments vary from field to field and hence are called "field-dependent", while other aspects of an argument are the same in all fields and hence are called "field-. - invariant." The vice of absolutism, Toulmin argues, lies in its failure to understand the aspect of argument that is field-dependent; absolutism assumes that all aspects of an argument are invariant to the field.

In Understanding Man (1972), Toulmin suggests that anthropologists were inclined to side with relativists because they noticed the influence of cultural variations on rational arguments. In other words, the anthropologist or relativist overemphasises the importance of the 'field-dependent' aspect of arguments and neglects or fails to recognise the 'field-invariant' elements. To find solutions to the problems of absolutism and relativism, Toulmin attempts throughout his work to develop standards that are neither absolutist nor relativist for assessing the value of ideas.

Pragma Dialectics. Researchers at the University of Amsterdam in the Netherlands were the first to develop a rigorous modern version of dialectics called pragma-dialectics. The intuitive idea is to formulate clear rules, adherence to which will lead to reasonable discussion and valid conclusions. Frans X. van Eemeren , the late Rob Grootendorst and many of their students and collaborators have produced a large number of papers explaining this idea.

The dialectical conception of rationality is given by ten rules for critical discussion, all of which are tools for resolving differences of opinion [128]. The theory postulates this as an ideal model, not something one would expect to find as an empirical fact. However, the model can serve as an important heuristic and critical tool to test how close reality comes to this ideal, and to point out where discourse goes wrong, that is, when rules are broken. Any such violation would constitute a fallacy. While pragma-dialectics does not focus primarily on fallacies, it offers a systematic approach to consistently addressing them.

Van Eemeren and Grothendorst identified four stages of argumentative dialogue. These stages can be seen as a protocol of argumentation. In a somewhat loose interpretation, the stages are as follows:

Confrontation stage: Presentation of a difference of opinion, such as a debate issue or political disagreement.

Initial stage: agreeing on material and procedural starting points, a mutually acceptable common ground of facts and beliefs, and the rules to be followed in the discussion (e.g., how evidence should be presented and defining closure conditions).

Argumentation stage: presenting arguments for and against the point of view under consideration by applying the principles of logic and common sense according to agreed rules.

Final stage: determining whether a viewpoint has withstood reasonable criticism and its acceptance is justified. This occurs when the conditions for completion are met (among them may be, for example, a time limit or the identification of an arbiter).

Van Eemeren and Grootendorst provide a detailed list of rules to be applied at each step of the protocol [128] Moreover, in these authors' description of argumentation, the protocol specifies certain roles of protagonist and antagonist that are determined by the conditions that create the need for argumentation.

## 1.2. Logical constructs.

Logical constructions are the specificity of algorithmic logic. As a generalisation of logical argumentation we can consider the studies of Douglas N. Walton. He developed a kind of philosophical theory of logical argumentation built on a set of practical methods or logical constructs that help the user to identify, analyse and evaluate arguments in everyday spoken discourse and in more structured domains such as debate, law and scientific fields [129, 130] There are four main components: argumentation schemes [131], dialogue structures, argument matching tools and formal argumentation systems. The method uses the notion of commitment in dialogue as the main tool for analysing and evaluating argumentation rather than the notion of persuasion [132]. Commitments are statements that an agent has expressed or formulated, committed to fulfil or publicly stated. According to the commitment model, agents interact with each other in a dialogue in which each in turn contributes speech acts. The dialogue structure uses critical questions as a way to test plausible explanations and to look for weaknesses in an argument that raise doubts about the acceptability of the argument.

Walton's model of logical argumentation held a view of evidence and justification different from the dominant epistemology of analytic philosophy, which was based on the justified structure of true beliefs [133] In the logical argumentation approach, knowledge is seen as a form of commitment to a belief, firmly anchored by an argumentation procedure that tests evidence on both sides and uses standards of proof to determine whether a proposition qualifies as knowledge. In this evidence-based approach, knowledge must be regarded as rebuttable.

In the logical approach, beliefs in argumentation are relegated to the background and logical information construction comes first [134]. In the logical approach, aspects of cognitive argumentation are excluded and communicative argumentation acts as an interview, i.e. as a clarifying factor.

Logic is one of the components of argumentation and is expressed as logical argumentation. Logic is the foundation of argumentation, but argumentation is a broader concept. Argumentation can use rhetoric and persuasion, which logic does not describe. The dominant role in argumentation is communication. Carl R. Wallace's seminal essay "The Essence of Rhetoric: Good Reasons" in the Quarterly Journal of Speech (1963) has prompted many scholars to study "marketplace argumentation"" - the ordinary arguments of ordinary people. The seminal essay on marketplace argumentation is Quarterly Journal of Speech (1967): "Logic and Marketplace Argumentation" by Ray Lynn Anderson and C. David Mortensen [135] This line of thinking led to a natural alliance with recent developments in the sociology of knowledge. Some scholars have linked it to recent developments in philosophy, Rorty calling this shift in emphasis a "linguistic turn".

In this new hybrid approach, argumentation is used with or without empirical evidence to draw convincing conclusions about questions that are moral, scientific, epistemological, or of a nature that science alone cannot answer. Out of pragmatism and many intellectual developments in the humanities and social sciences grew "non-philosophical" theories of argumentation that placed the formal and material bases of arguments in particular intellectual domains. These theories include informal logic, social epistemology, ethnomethodology, speech acts, sociology of knowledge, sociology of science, and social psychology. These new theories are not illogical or anti-logical. They find logical coherence in most discourse communities. Thus, these theories are often referred to as "sociological" theories because they focus on the social foundations of knowledge. To summarise, logic is part of argumentation, but does not replace it.

A logical construct can be a construction or analysis tool. logical construct is a subspecies of information construct [136]

Russellian logical constructions are fairly rigid models. They differ in whether they include explicit definitions or contextual definitions, and in the degree to which their result should be described as showing or qualitative.

Here we should note the difference between logical constructions and constructions. Logical constructions, logical formulas result have oppositional variables [137, 138] "true", "false". They give an unambiguous result. Logical constructions result have either showing, reference, or dichotomous [139, 140] but not oppositional. They give a multi-ambiguous result that requires content.

For quite a long time, logical constructions have included the special technique of contextual definition. In contextual definition, obvious singular terms (either definite descriptions or class terms) are excluded using the rules for defining the entire sentence in which they occur. Constructions like those using contextual definitions are usually called "incomplete symbols", and constructions like class theory are usually called "fictions". It would be a mistake to regard Russell's logical constructions as the product of the backward operation of a method beginning with logical analysis. Analysis was indeed the distinctive method of Russell's realist and atomistic philosophy, and the method of construction came only later

Definite descriptions are the logical constructs that Russell has in mind when he describes them as "incomplete symbols". Other constructs, such as the concepts of area and range relations and of reciprocal-valued mappings, which are crucial to the development of arithmetic, are "incomplete" only in an indirect sense, since they are defined as classes of a certain sort, which in turn are constructions Russell's theory of descriptions introduces two logical forms of propositions: definite descriptions and indefinite descriptions. Russell's introduction of definite descriptions is an example of the philosophical distinction between a surface grammatical form and a logical form. It marked the beginning of linguistic analysis as a method in philosophy

## 2. Expanding the scope of the concept of algorithm

In algorithmic logic an algorithm is used in a broader sense than in calculations. Algorithm is used in calculations, in mathematical calculations in mathematics, in solving applied problems. Algorithm is applied: in information interpretation, in cognitive modelling, in virtual modelling, in mixed reality systems, in the operation of computing networks and distributed systems. Algorithms are applied in logical inference systems, in intelligent systems, in reasoning systems, in verification methods, in coding/decoding methods, in information retrieval systems, in control and decision-making systems

Algorithm (in the narrow sense) is a prescription that defines a sequence of actions that provides the required result from the initial data. This technological definition does not correspond to the modern application of an algorithm. In a broad sense, an algorithm is a sequence of actions not only in the field of calculations, but also to describe the regularities of the information field and the development of society. An important new property of an algorithm is its application to describe regularities in the information field and in information situations. Algorithms are considered as a tool for obtaining explicit knowledge from implicit knowledge. Hence algorithm can be considered as a means of cognition, which confirms education. Furthermore, in stochastic systems, algorithm [141] is applied as a means of systematisation and pattern building. Algorithms are applied in group activities. In particular, when controlling groups of robots. They consider actions not only in technical systems, but also in living organisms or living systems. This describes an algorithm as a means of describing self-organisation and stability. Algorithms are used in medicine (diagnostic algorithm) [142]. This describes an algorithm as a means of describing information interaction and decision making.

Algorithms in education are used: in designing educational activities, in teaching and knowledge transfer, and in testing. This describes an algorithm as a systematised means of knowledge transfer. Algorithms are used to test subjects and to assess the difficulty of tasks. This gives reason to consider an algorithm a means of identifying latent variables and latent knowledge. The concept of algorithm is used in financial evaluation of investment activities [143]. This gives reason to consider algorithm a schematic technique of qualitatively quantitative evaluation. In the field of computation, an algorithm is used in two qualities: procedurally for finding solutions and descriptively for describing the finding of a solution. A computational algorithm, as a tool for finding a solution, is often associated with numerical methods. This gives reason to consider the algorithm as a numerical method for obtaining solutions, in conditions where it is impossible to obtain a solution by analytical methods. A computational algorithm, as a method describing the finding of a solution, is related to analytical methods. This gives reason to consider the algorithm as an analytical method of obtaining solutions. There is a concept of statistical algorithm [144, 145]. This is a direction of calculations in numerical methods, when, if it is impossible to obtain an analytical description, statistical data are used and the phenomenon or object is analysed on their basis. Statistical algorithms and numerical algorithms should be considered as a tool for processing unstructured and complex information. The development of statistical algorithms is logical-statistical algorithms [146]. Analysis shows that this term denotes methods that include qualitative analysis, which is modelled by a certain logic. This gives reason to consider the algorithm a method of qualitative analysis, in conditions when it is impossible to obtain a solution by numerical methods alone.

An algorithm can be considered as a technological system and as a complex system if it has the features of integrity and completeness. In this case, the methods of system analysis can be applied to the algorithm, and the algorithm itself can be considered as a complex technological system. To summarise briefly, we can state that an algorithm can be considered as a converter of qualitative and quantitative information.

An algorithm can be considered as an information model. An algorithm is a dual information model. As a description it is a descriptive descriptive model, as a procedural object it is a prescriptive model or a procedural model. An algorithm from the perspective of information asymmetry is a mechanism that eliminates information asymmetry and information uncertainty. However, this quality of algorithms has been little applied so far. Within the framework of the information approach it is possible to replace the notion of problem solving condition by the term information situation. The conditions for solving the problem and the conditions for applying the algorithm are a fixed parameter at the beginning of the solution. Information situation is a dynamic concept, as it describes initial and subsequent conditions of algorithm application. There is also little use of the systems approach to analyse algorithms as a complex system.

Algorithm is widely used in computer science and mathematics in solving a variety of applied problems [147-150]. Initially, an algorithm was treated as an information construct for performing calculations. An algorithm (in the narrow sense) is a prescription defining a sequence of actions that provides the required result from the initial data [151]. This is a technological definition. Let us give two incorrect examples.

*Wikipedia* [152]. An algorithm is interpreted as a set of precisely defined rules for solving some class of problems or a set of instructions describing the order of actions for solving a certain problem. The term instruction requires rigid binding of an algorithm to a prescriptive model. Independent instructions can be executed in any order, in parallel, if it is possible and increases computational performance.

*Humanitarian Portal* [153]. Algorithm is a precisely defined prescription for performing in a certain order some sequence of operations unambiguously leading to the solution of a particular problem.

Obviously, the above definitions refer only to deterministic algorithms and do not describe a whole range of algorithms, including situational, organisational subsidiarity and multi-agent algorithms.

Qualitatively, we can distinguish computational, control and interpretive - algorithms.

Computational algorithms have logical constructs as their basis and convert input data into output using computational functions.

Control algorithms have semantic (heuristic) and logical constructs as a basis and transform input decision conditions into a set of alternatives on the basis of analytical and computational functions.

Interpretive algorithms have as a basis the revealed regularities of the surrounding world or information field and transform objective regularities into sets of algorithmic constructions or paradigms.

The semantics of control algorithms may differ significantly from the logic of computational algorithms. It includes the issuance of necessary control actions at given moments of time or as a reaction to external events. A control algorithm can remain correct with infinite execution at unchanged external situation. From the control perspective, the algorithm realises the axiom of choice. The axiom of choice is a principle of set theory, according to which for any family of non-empty sets there exists a choice function, which puts one element of each set in correspondence with its element

Besides computing, algorithms are used in other areas: in information interpretation [154-156], in cognitive modelling [157], in virtual modelling [158, 159], in the operation of distributed systems [160], in logical inference methods, in game theory, in reasoning methods, in verification methods [161], in coding/decoding methods, in information retrieval methods [162, 163], in describing the operation of information systems, and in control and decision-making methods.

In a broad sense, an algorithm has come to be called a sequence of actions not only in the field of computation, but also to describe the regularities of the information field and the development of society [164]. This approach describes an algorithm as a means that reveals the regularity of mass systems. Algorithms are seen as a means of knowledge acquisition [165]. This describes the algorithm as a means of cognition. Algorithms as systematised processes are considered in jurisprudence [166]. This describes the algorithm as a means of systematisation and establishing patterns. Algorithms are used in the study of group activity and corporate governance [167-170]. This describes an algorithm as a means of systematising group activities. This considers activities not only in technical systems but also in living organisms or living systems [171-174]. This describes the algorithm as a means of describing self-organisation and sustainability. Algorithms are used in medicine (diagnostic algorithm) [142, 175]. This describes an algorithm as a means of describing information interaction and decision making.

Algorithms are used in education [176-180]. At that, it is used in different qualities. Algorithm is used for organisation and design of educational activity, for teaching and transfer of knowledge by a teacher. Algorithm is used in acquiring knowledge by a student, and in testing [181-185]. Algorithms are applied in the study of patterns of connection between the results of education and pre-professional training. Collectively describes an algorithm as a systematised means of knowledge transfer. Almost all types of testing use a variety of sets of algorithms. This describes the algorithm as a comprehensive means of assessing the state of the object of analysis. In education, an algorithm based on Item Response Theory [186, 187] or on the well-known Rasch model [188] is widely used. Item Response Theory (IRT) [187, 189, 190] is mainly used in pedagogical measurements [191] as well as in structural modelling [192]. This approach is used not only for testing subjects, but also for assessing task difficulty. This gives reason to consider the algorithm a means of identifying latent variables and latent knowledge. The concept of algorithm is used in financial evaluation of investment activities [193]. This gives a reason to consider algorithm a schematic technique of qualitatively quantitative evaluation. In the field of computation, an algorithm is used in two qualities: procedurally for finding solutions and descriptively for describing the finding of a solution. A computational algorithm as a tool for finding a solution is often associated with numerical methods. This gives reason to consider the algorithm as a numerical method of obtaining solutions, in conditions when it is impossible to obtain a solution by analytical methods. Computational algorithm as a method describing finding a solution, [194] is related to analytical methods. This gives reason to consider the algorithm as an analytical method of obtaining solutions. There is a concept of statistical algorithm. This is a direction of calculations in numerical methods, when, when it is impossible to obtain an analytical description, statistical data are used and the phenomenon or object is analysed on their basis. Statistical algorithms and numerical algorithms should be considered as a tool for processing unstructured and complex information.

The development of statistical algorithms is logical-statistical algorithms [144]. Analysis shows that this term denotes methods that include qualitative analysis [146], which is modelled by a certain logic. This gives reason to consider the algorithm method of qualitative analysis [195], in conditions when it is impossible to obtain a solution by numerical methods alone.

An algorithm can be considered as a system if it has the features of integrity and completeness. In this case, the methods of system analysis can be applied to the algorithm, and the algorithm itself can be considered as a complex technological system [196]. To summarise briefly, we can state that an algorithm can be considered as a converter of qualitative and quantitative information.

An algorithm is a multi-dimensional object. At the same time, it has been very little compared and treated as an information model. An algorithm is a dual information model. As a description it is a descriptive model [197], as a procedural object it is a prescriptive model [198]. An algorithm from the information interaction perspective is a mechanism that eliminates information asymmetry [199-202] and information uncertainty [203-205]. However, from these positions, algorithms have been little considered so far. Within the framework of the modern information approach, it is reasonable to replace the concepts of problem solving conditions and algorithm application conditions by the term information situation. The conditions for solving a problem and the conditions for applying an algorithm are a one-time parameter, at the moment when the solution starts. The information situation is a dynamic concept. It describes the initial conditions and has the possibility of transformation or adaptation to changing conditions and can describe the situation from the beginning to its completion of the solution. There is also little use of the systems approach to analyse algorithms as a complex system.

According to the computational trajectory, algorithms are divided into direct (single trajectory) or algorithms of the first kind [206-208] and algorithms of the second kind [209, 210] (multi-trajectory). Algorithms of the first kind are graph transport, have a definite computation trajectory (with many possible trajectories) and are implemented on a deterministic Turing machine. Algorithms of the second kind contain uncertainty. They contain a set of computational trajectories and are implemented on a deterministic Turing machine.

## 2.1. System properties of the algorithm

An algorithm can be an open and a closed system. A pass-through algorithm is a closed system. An iterative algorithm is an open system. It can have system properties. Straightforward algorithms can be considered as complex systems and a systems approach can be applied to their analysis. As a system, an algorithm is a closed system. As a system, an algorithm has systemic properties. This gives grounds to distinguish system and functional characteristics of algorithms. This gives grounds to introduce the concept of "algorithmic system" and "logical-algorithmic system" (LAS). The following system properties are applied in modern algorithms.

*The principle of connectedness.* It consists in the fact that the processes of an algorithm can be described as a system with a set of elements and links between them.

*Functionality principle.* It consists in the fact that the algorithm solves not only logical problems, but carries out functional processing of information in accordance with a set of functions.

*The principle of integrity.* It consists in the fact that the algorithm is an integral system and the exclusion of at least one element of the algorithm violates the integrity and does not give the necessary result.

*Principle of structuredness.* It means the presence of algorithm structure as a mandatory property. Functional characteristics of algorithms are related to their performance, adaptability versatility or specialisation. By functional similarity, an algorithm can be compared to a network system or a network.

The simplest algorithmic system $S$ can be represented as a mechanism for transforming *an* input set $X$ into an output set $Y$.

$$S: X \rightarrow Y \quad (2.1).$$

By analogy, the $AL$ algorithm can be represented as a mechanism *for* converting input data $X$ into output data $Y$.

$$AL: X \rightarrow Y \quad (2.2).$$

## 2.2. Knowledge extraction

From the perspective of knowledge extraction, an algorithm is a means for knowledge extraction. Another relatively new term used in the theory of algorithms as information transformers is the term "externalisation". It means the transformation of implicit informalised knowledge into explicit formalised knowledge. This term was introduced by the Japanese scientist Noyaka, in his famous paper [211]. Implicit knowledge requires its identification and transformation of implicit knowledge [212-214] into explicit knowledge. The ideas of knowledge transformation are developed in [214]. This term correlates as a private term with the notion of knowledge extraction.

From the point of view of knowledge externalisation, an algorithm is a means of knowledge transformation. An algorithm is a mechanism for transforming one form of knowledge (problem condition) into another form of knowledge (problem solution). In his work, Noyaka describes a four-step algorithm that solves four qualitatively different transformations.

In ordinary computing, the algorithm solves one qualitative problem. It transforms initial conditions into a solution. As a rule, it is either an algorithm of the first kind only (direct solution) or an algorithm of the second kind (step-by-step solution).

In the four-stage scheme [211], Nonaka describes jointly algorithms of the first and second kind, although he does not use such terms. An algorithm can be referred to the class of closed deterministic complex systems. An algorithm can be considered as a functional system because it always performs a certain function. The functional description of complex systems was investigated by Mesarovic [38]. Therefore, we can use the formalism proposed by him to describe algorithms.

Algorithms have stable relationships and refer to systems with a constant structure. The description of an algorithm can be considered as explicit knowledge, which is perceived by different people and can be transferred from one person to another. A set of algorithms solving related problems makes it possible to make a scientific generalisation that goes beyond a single technical solution to the problem, just as a single chess game gives reason to generalise the theory of chess playing. This gives reason to link algorithms to knowledge acquisition.

It is well known that people are potentially capable of perceiving approximately the same amount of information. However, the conclusions that subjects draw from the same portions of information are different. This creates contradictions and the need to find compromises. In contrast to subjects, algorithms, on the basis of identical portions of information, obtain identical results. From this point of view, algorithms can be considered as a mechanism that is able to find compromises and resolve contradictions.

## 2.3. Trinitarian methodology

It is incorrect to reduce an algorithm to an implicative relation. The systemological aspect of an algorithm allows us to consider it as an inference system or as a tool for knowledge extraction [89, 90]. An algorithm can be considered as a basis for qualitative reasoning if it relies on qualitative characteristics. The simplest inference and decision making is based on the rule "If A, then B". This means that if there is an informational situation [215-221] in which. if "A" as a condition of actions, then action "B" should be taken, which gives the result "C". Such a solution is called a simple solution and is described by a trinitarian scheme or double implication.

$A{\to}B{\to}C.$ (2.3)

Such decision chains occur in simple situations, such as in directive control [221-225], where the occurrence of situation "A" is stipulated by a regulation or normative. In such a regulation, action "B" for situation "A" is prescribed to produce outcome "C". In practice, there is a need to verify the outcome. This leads to the trinitarian model [226, 227] "goal - method - result". This is depicted by the diagram shown in Fig.2.1. In this aspect, the algorithm can be considered as a prescriptive information model. At the same time, it should be noted that the elementary link of the algorithm has elements of the triad or trinitarian model [228-230].

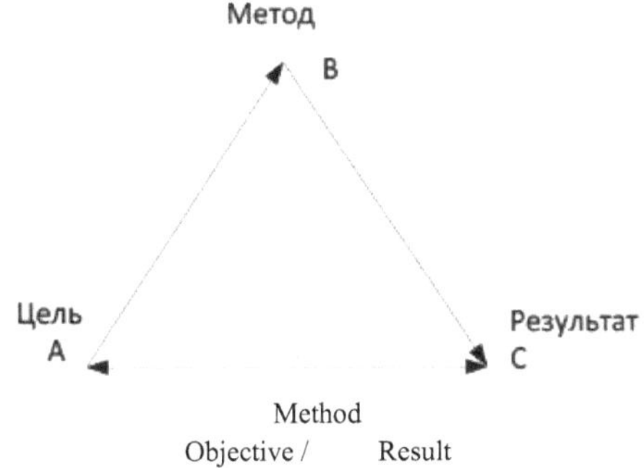


Fig.2.1. Trinitarian model of the direct algorithm.

The scheme in Fig. 2.1 shows that the calculation is not the end of the algorithm. An important and obligatory stage is the verification of the solution - the segment AC or the relation between the vertices AC. In the aspect of the logic of cognition, one more property of the algorithm can be noted. An algorithm transforms one kind of knowledge into another and actually creates explicit knowledge (result) on the basis of implicit knowledge (conditions or situation). This gives grounds to consider the algorithm as a tool of externalisation [231, 232] of knowledge.

## 2.4.Sequences.

Among the many algorithms, there are those that can be viewed as logical sequences [233-237]. Such sequences are called sequences, and algorithms are called sequential [238, 239]. Many sequential iterative algorithms can be parallelised directly by identifying dependencies between input objects. This approach yields many simple and practical parallel algorithms, but there are still problems in achieving performance efficiency and high parallelism.

An algorithm as a logical progression is used most often in computing. A block diagram of such an algorithm is an example of a logical construction. Such an algorithm solves several tasks. The first task: justifying the logic of the investigation or computation. The second task: knowledge acquisition. Third task: transformation of implicit knowledge into explicit knowledge. Fourth task: establishing the regularity of the information field or pattern of development. The fifth task is a sequential search of variants in order to choose the optimal one out of many. It is widely used in discrete mathematics. The sixth task of an algorithm as a logical sequence is justification of scientific research, fixing it in the form of a stable scheme, available for repetition and verification. The seventh task transformation of information into information resources [240]. The eighth task is the transformation of input data into the result of calculations. The ninth task is pattern recognition based on a set of patterns [241]. The tenth task is to divide a set of parameters into two classes using a separating hyperplane [242] and many other tasks [243-246].

An algorithm as a logical sequence or sequences solves procedural tasks step by step, step by step. Procedural or prescriptive tasks consist in the fact that on the basis of a set of facts, or initial information situation, the process of calculation in a computational information situation is realised and a result describing the final information situation is obtained. Algorithm schemes are constructed on the basis of logical succession (Fig. 2.2).

The basis for constructing an algorithm as a logical sequence is a task, which in relation to an information situation (situation) acquires facts and specific conditions.

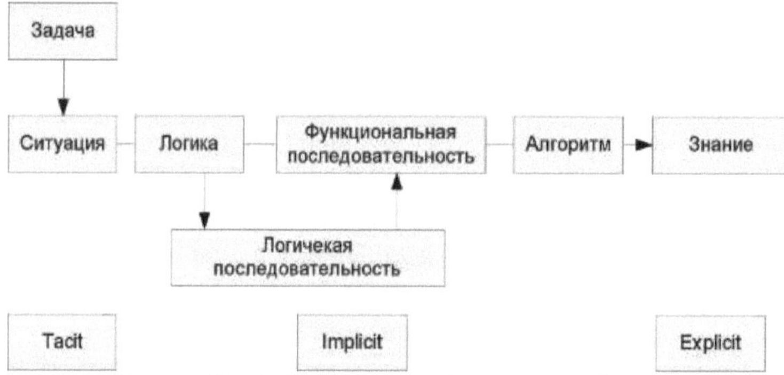


Fig.2.2. Scheme of logical succession when constructing an algorithm.

On the basis of the task conditions and the logic (logics) applied, a logical sequence is constructed, which is the basis of an algorithm. The logical sequence serves as the basis for the construction of a functional sequence, which serves as the basis for calculations or other analyses. Algorithm as a logical sequence includes two components logical and functional. This is its peculiarity and difference from "purely" logical sequences.

In essence, a functional shell is put on the logical basis of an algorithm. An important distinction of an algorithm as a logical sequence is knowledge operations. At the initial stage of constructing a logical sequence there is implicit knowledge (tacit), which is not formalisable and not transferable. Then at the stage of formalisation the tacit knowledge is transformed into another form of tacit knowledge (implicit). As a result of algorithm functioning, explicit knowledge is extracted.

*Factual statements* occupy an intermediate position between identically true statements (tautologies), on the one hand, and always identically false statements, on the other. For algorithms, such statements can occur. Their conclusions can be either true or false, depending on the facts on which their premises rely. While the truth of tautologies or the falsity of contradictions can be established by a purely logical analysis of these statements, the truth value of factual statements requires an appeal to facts. In order to establish the truth or falsity of factual statements, it is necessary to investigate the functional connections and information relations that serve as premises of factual conclusions. On this basis, factual statements are often also called *empirical* statements, as opposed to analytical statements in logic and mathematics.

The original definition of an algorithm cannot be considered strict, due to its versatile application and interpretation. Nowadays, due to the wide use of algorithms, it is convenient to designate it by the term information construction, which reflects the variety of forms and types of algorithm. Algorithm as a logical following is convenient for describing regularities.

An important distinction of an algorithm as a logical sequence is knowledge operations. At the initial stage of constructing a logical sequence, there is tacit knowledge (tacit), which is not formalisable or transferable. Then at the stage of formalisation the implicit knowledge is transformed into another form of implicit knowledge (implicit). As a result of algorithm functioning, explicit knowledge is extracted.

### 3.  Pass-through and iterative algorithms

Any verified logical chain of inference can be a computational algorithm. Such a chain can be the basis for decision making. Such a chain can be the basis of analysis. In all cases we can apply the notion of an algorithm: a computational algorithm, a decision-making algorithm, an analysis algorithm. For these cases, the structure of the algorithm as a sequence is important. Algorithms fall into different categories. One division is related to the sequence of problem solving. Algorithms that allow solving a problem sequentially without interruptions and human participation are called direct algorithms or end-to-end algorithms [208]. Tasks that allow to obtain an end-to-end continuous solution are called tasks of the first kind. Accordingly, algorithms for solving these problems are called so [247].

Algorithms of linear, branching and cyclic structure are distinguished by the nature of connections between the stages of calculations. A linear algorithm is an algorithm in which operations are performed sequentially. A branching algorithm is an algorithm in which the path of computation depends on certain conditions or computational situation. A cyclic algorithm is an algorithm in which the same operations are repeatedly performed according to a given condition.

An algorithm has a structure - this is its obligatory property. The structure of an algorithm usually reflects the logical relationship between input and output data and is described by topological models. The topological model of an algorithm of the first kind is a transport graph. It has one input and usually one output. There are special algorithms that can have a finite number of outputs corresponding to variants of the problem solution. Each output usually means obtaining a qualitatively different result.

The structure of a complex algorithm has similarities with network systems, which gives reason to use network theory to analyse algorithms. For example, routing in a network is used to find the optimal solution in a complex algorithm. A route in a complex algorithm is a solution. Structurally, a complex algorithm can be viewed as a network. The qualitative difference between an algorithm and a network is that a network is a relatively homogeneous system in which the same types of information flows, corresponding to a single network protocol, function.

In an algorithm as a network system, the quality of the information flow changes at each processing step. Another difference is the quality of vertices of the network and the algorithm. In a network all vertices have one quality, in an algorithm intermediate vertices have two qualities: state and condition.

An algorithm has a functional purpose and fulfils certain functions. This gives grounds to compare it with a functional system. Direct algorithms correspond to the characteristics of a complex closed system and can be described by the formalism of general systems theory. The peculiarity of direct algorithms is that they do not function independently, but require a computing environment. This necessitates the adaptation of algorithms to the computing environment.

The peculiarity of algorithms as systems is that they require testing and verification before they can be applied. As a system, an algorithm belongs to the class of technological systems. A technological system is always connected or placed inside a technical or organisational system. Therefore, the effectiveness of an algorithm depends on the properties of the technical system within which it operates.

Problems of the second kind are those for which the solution cannot be obtained in one pass or in one cycle. This type of problems and algorithms is also used in computing systems. Problems of the second kind are also those for which it is necessary to apply a nondeterministic Turing machine. In problems of the second kind, the solution is obtained sequentially by partially solving the problem at one stage and then heuristically selecting the further part of the solution. Between the solution stages, natural intelligence is involved.

An example of tasks and algorithms of the second kind is a chess game. In the initial state of a chess game, the information situation is such that it is impossible to say which of the opponents will win and how the game will end. It is impossible to say this to an observer from the outside and to each of the players. Initially each player has equal chances. But in the process of the game, each player makes a decision not as an automaton, but taking into account information about the opponent's style of play, about his psychophysical state and so on. These implicit and intuitive knowledge the player transforms into real actions. That is why in such situations intuitionistic logic is used as one of the methods. When players start to make the first moves information uncertainty decreases. The situation becomes clearer for each of the players and for an outside observer. However, the time factor starts to work. The solution must be obtained within the time allowed by the rules.

Each move of a chess game can be considered as a stage of solving a problem of the second kind. The more moves, the closer is the end of the game, i.e. the solution of this problem. The value of the result of a chess game is private for each of the players and general for the experience of the game and the accumulation of knowledge about the methods of play. Similarly, the solution of problems of the second kind has a general value.

Solutions of complex evolutionary problems of the second kind allow us to accumulate experience in problem solving and cognition of the world. It is in this aspect that the algorithm is considered in the monograph "Developmental Algorithms" by Academician N. Moiseev. N. Moiseev uses the term "algorithm" in an extended sense, not as a computational mechanism, but as a means of solving complex problems and cognition of the world.

The topological description of an algorithm is a tuple $< VF, A, VT>$, where $VF$ is the set of condition vertices , $VA$ is the set of result vertices, $A$ is the set of functional arcs. The first vertex of the algorithm is always a condition. The last vertex of the algorithm is always a result. Intermediate vertices can be considered by two factors: result and conditions. For the next step a vertex is a condition. For the previous step a vertex is a result.

In terms of topological structure, an algorithm can be compared to a network system or a network.

Direct algorithms are divided into simple and complex, cyclic and acyclic, single-route and multi-route. A simple single-route, acyclic algorithm has the form of a linear chain (Fig. 3.1).

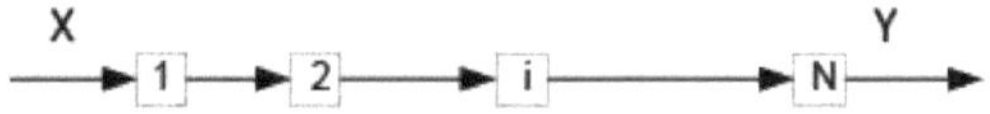

Figure 3.1. Simple end-to-end or direct algorithm

A simple end-to-end algorithm has only one computation path. The structural complexity of such an algorithm depends on the number of nodes (states) and the complexity of transitions (computational operations) between nodes. The peculiarity of a computational algorithm is the accumulation of errors. If errors are possible at the stages of computation, the more stages there are, the larger the final error is $\Delta$

$$\Delta = \Sigma \delta i, \ i=1...N \ (4)$$

Here N is the number of stages of the algorithm, Si is the calculation error of the *i-th* stage

The computation time Tv also depends on the number of steps. Approximate formula

$$T_B = \Sigma ti, \ i=1...N \ (5)$$

Here N is the number of stages of the algorithm, *ti* is the processing time at the *i-th* stage. The disadvantage of the algorithm in the scheme of Fig. 3.1 is the impossibility of obtaining high accuracy of calculations when using approximate calculations.

To improve the accuracy or iterative calculations, cyclic algorithms, algorithms with correction are used. The scheme of a simple cyclic algorithm is shown in

Fig. 3.2.

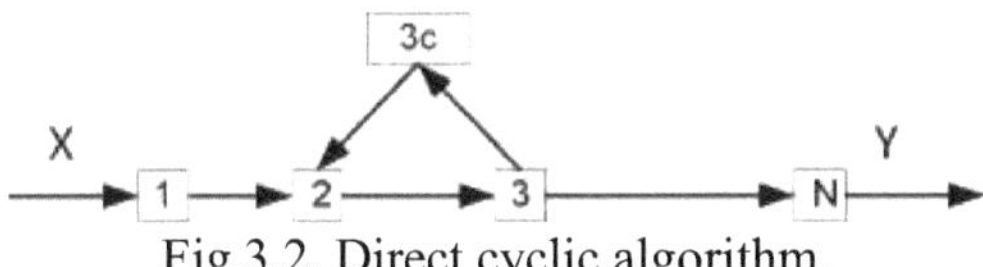

Fig.3.2. Direct cyclic algorithm.

Such an algorithm is called an algorithm with a cycle, which follows from the theory of topology. Vertices 2, 3, 3c form a closed trinitary system. It should be noted that the cycle in the simplest model is a trinitary system. Correction, verification, redesign are possible in this loop. Therefore, schemes of this kind are used in design and are called design with correction. The disadvantage of the algorithm in the scheme of Fig. 3 is the possible instability of calculations.

When solving complex multivariate problems, complex algorithms with network control and complex links are used. An example scheme of such class of algorithms is shown in Fig. 3.3.

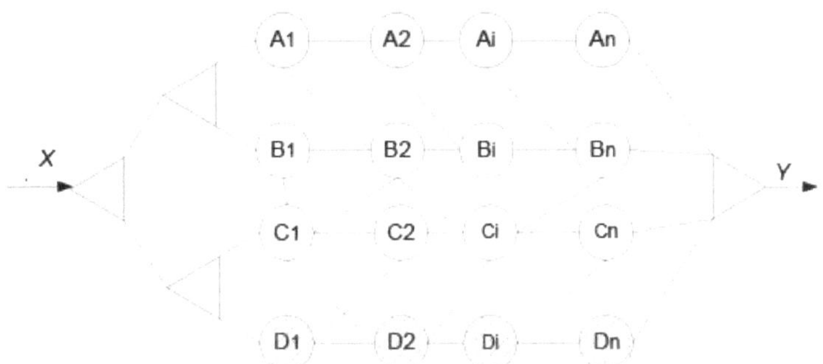

Figure 3.3. Complex direct algorithm

The algorithm scheme in Fig. 3.3 represents a typical transport graph. The disadvantage of the algorithm in the scheme of Fig. 3.3 is the possible instability of computational optimisation. There may be a group of alternative solution routes. These are solutions that traverse different nodes of the graph but lead to the same result. However, all of them have different computation time (5) and different total errors (4).

The consideration of algorithm as a technological component in information processing is reflected in the famous work by T. Kormen, published in 1990 and repeatedly reprinted. This work lays down the canonical foundations for constructing only computational algorithms of the first kind. The first basic principle of algorithm construction according to T. Kormen is the heuristic principle of "divide and conquer". In fact, it is an algorithm of the second kind using qualitative analysis. That is, T. Komen uses the second kind of algorithm to construct the first kind of algorithm.

The scheme of the algorithm of the second kind is shown in Fig.3.4.

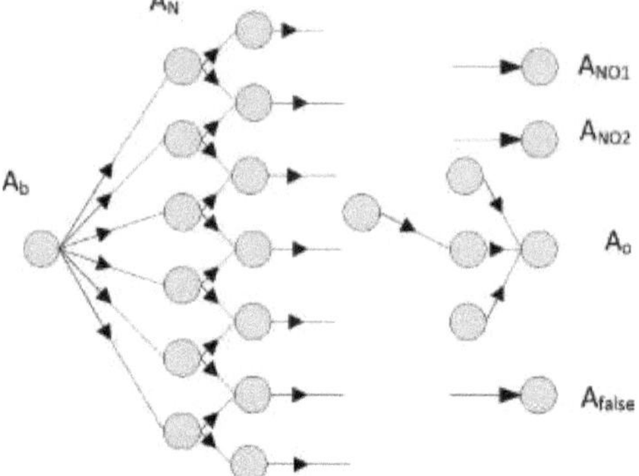



Fig.3.4. Algorithm of the second kind.

In Fig. 3.4, the initial state of the solution corresponds to vertex $A_b$ . The situation of uncertainty occurs at the level of vertices $AN$ . As a result of the solution, it is possible to obtain optimal solutions $AO$ , suboptimal solutions $A_{NO1}$ $A_{NO2}$ , AND even erroneous solutions $Af_{iase}$ . This also distinguishes a problem of the second kind from problems of the first kind in which there is a single solution. In problems of the second kind there can be many solutions including optimal and suboptimal ones.

## 4. Algorithmic complexity

There are different types of complexity. Algorithmic complexity is one of the types of complexity. The concepts of complexity theory and algorithmic complexity theory should be separated. Algorithmic complexity theory is a subset of complexity theory and is primarily concerned with computation and computational complexity. Algorithmic information processing corresponds to the transformation of input information (input data) into a processing result. In computation, an algorithm mediates the transformation of information. In modern understanding, an algorithm is a broader concept than a computation scheme. There are algorithms for development of cognition algorithms search algorithms [248], recognition algorithms [249], identification algorithms [250], separation algorithms, e.g. by hyperplane method [242], knowledge management algorithms (KM Algorithm) [250], multi-agent algorithms [251-253] and others. Experience in information processing shows that two types of algorithms can be distinguished by the type of obtaining solutions: algorithms of the first kind algorithms of the second kind. With the algorithm of the first kind, the solution of the problem can be obtained with a single computational sequence. Fig. 4.1 shows a generalised algorithm of the first kind

Fig.4.1. Generalised algorithm of the first kind

All algorithms of the first kind are characterised by one input and one output. All first-order algorithms can be simplified into a single block with an input (X) and an output (Y). Most algorithms of the first kind involve solutions to problems that can be solved by a deterministic Turing machine (DTM) with limited time or space resources. Many algorithms of the second kind involve solutions to problems that can be solved by a non-deterministic Turing machine (NTM).

To estimate complexity, the concept of "Time Complexity Class" is often used, which is evaluated by the time resources required to solve the problem. To estimate complexity, the following procedures are most often used: estimate the time cost of running a given algorithm; compare two algorithms and assign them either to the same or to different classes. We consider the complexity classes of algorithms. as a set of algorithms that solve commensurate computational problems. A complexity class is usually determined by three factors: the type of computational problem, the model of computation, and the limited computational resource. For example, the complexity class P is defined as the set of problems whose solutions can be obtained by a deterministic Turing machine in polynomial time.

**Asymptotic complexity**

In a simple interpretation, a computational problem or a computational task can be represented as a question formulated in a formal language that a computer can answer. In this aspect with computational problem and computational complexity comes the notion of information language [107, 254]. The notions of "problem" and "language" are largely synonymous in computability and algorithmic complexity theory. A Turing machine is usually understood as a machine that defines a language. Related to computational complexity is the notion of a computational model. A computational model, in turn, is related to computational resources: 'time', 'memory'. In algorithmic complexity theory, complexity classes are defined by the resource requirements of the algorithm, rather than physical resource requirements. The main computational model in algorithmic complexity theory is the Turing machine, although other models are also used. In a Turing machine, instead of using standard information units of time (second), the information units used are the number of elementary steps required to solve the problem. A Turing machine, instead of using standard information units of volume (bytes), uses information units like the number of cells that are used on the machine's tape.

The running time of a single algorithm may vary for different input data, both in terms of the quality of the data set and in terms of volume. To estimate the complexity of an algorithm, one usually considers the time complexity, which specifies the maximum amount of time required for the input data. This approach leads to the notion of asymptotic complexity [255]. Less common is, average complexity, which is the average time taken for input data of a certain size. In these cases, time complexity is usually expressed as a function of the size of the input data [256]. Since this function is usually difficult to compute accurately, and the execution time of small input data is usually irrelevant, one usually focuses on the behaviour of complexity as the size of the input data increases, i.e., the asymptotic behaviour of complexity. Asymptotic complexity, which has the following varieties, is used to comparatively evaluate the complexity of algorithms

1. $f(n) \in O(g(n))$ - $f$ is bounded from above by the function $g$ (up to a constant multiplier) asymptotically

$\exists(C>0),n_0 : \forall(n>n_0)\ |f(n)| \leq C|g(n)|$ или $\exists(C>0),n_0 : \forall(n>n_0)\ |(n) \leq Cg(n)$

2. $f(n) \in \Omega g(n))$ - - f is bounded from below by the function g (with accuracy up to a constant multiplier) asymptotically

$\exists(C>0),n0 : \forall(n>n0)\ |f(n)| \geq C|g(n)|$

3. $f(n) \in \Theta g(n))$ - f is bounded from above and below by the function g (up to a constant multiplier) asymptotically

$\exists(C, C'>0),n0 : \forall(n>n0)\ C|g(n)| \leq |f(n)| \leq C'|g(n)|$

4. $f(n) \in o\ g(n))$ - g dominates f asymptotically

$\forall(C>0),\ \exists n0 : \forall(n>n0)\ |f(n)| < C|g(n)|$

5. $f(n) \in \omega g(n))$ - f dominates g asymptotically

$\forall(C>0),\ \exists n0 : \forall(n>n0)\ |f(n)| > C|g(n)|$

6. $f(n) \sim g(n))$ - g is equivalent or *commensuratef* asymptotically

$lim\ f(n)/g(n)=1$

For asymptotic estimation we use the notation: big O, which is used to express an upper bound on the running time of an algorithm. Big *O is* one of the mathematical notations called *asymptotic notation*, which is used to express the behaviour of a function when its argument increases to infinity. The big *O* was used by the mathematician Paul Bachmann in the late 19th century, but is sometimes called the *Landau symbol* (mathematician, Edmund Landau) It is used to describe the constraint from above (see n1 above). The big omega is used to describe the constraint from below (see n2 above).

**Types of computational complexity of algorithms**

Different types of complexity of algorithms are distinguished. The traditional one uses time complexity as a basis, which is called computational complexity. Relating computational complexity to computation time. The computation time is denoted by *T(n)*. Time complexity is usually expressed using the capital letter O: *O(n), O(n log(n)), O($n^a$ ), O($2^n$ )* and others, where n is the size of the input data in bits *1odd required* for the representation. For example, an algorithm with time complexity is a *linear time algorithm* and an algorithm with time complexity for some constant a >1 is an *algorithm with polynomial time*

Let us consider algorithms of the first kind. It should be noted that different authors allow contradictory interpretations of the complexity of these algorithms. Therefore, let us consider examples and try to justify the complexity of some algorithms. The simplest algorithm is the constant time algorithm. This algorithm performs an operation in a fixed time regardless of the input data.All machine commands are constant time algorithms, denoted by *0(1)*. Fig.4.2 shows the constant time algorithm on the example of addition operation.

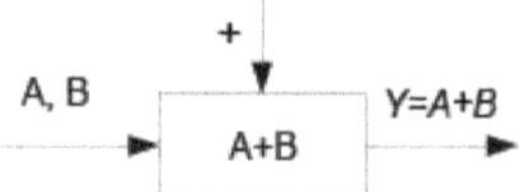



Fig.4.2 Constant time algorithm

Fig.4.2 is a complete realisation of the circuit in Fig.4.1. The constant time algorithm corresponds to the direct algorithm. The input data is a bounded set A, B. The condition represents a single operation, in this case addition. In general, it can be any operation with fixed time. The output represents the result of the operation or the sum. It should be noted that the time of the operation in the scheme of Fig. 4.2 depends on the type of data. Operations with integers are faster than with real numbers. Operations with real numbers are faster than with double precision numbers.

Some authors call the constant time algorithm an algorithm for calculating the mean. This is formally acceptable, but physically incorrect. The time of calculating the mean depends on the volume of the sample or array in which the mean is determined. Therefore, such an algorithm has a conditionally constant calculation time. Its time depends on the sample size, on the required accuracy of calculations, as well as on the types of input data. This example can be used to emphasise the conditionality of some types of complexity. It consists in the fact that algorithms that belong to the same class or type of complexity physically use different computation times.

*O(n)* linear time algorithms are used as an alternative to this algorithm. The algorithm for computing the mean is linear time algorithms. If we consider non-computational algorithms, the linear time algorithm is an algorithm of the first kind in the formulation of the task or problem (Fig. 4.3)

Fig.4.3: The linear time algorithm "idea-solution".

The solution can be a project, innovative development, managerial decision and so on. It is fundamental that the more blocks there are, the longer the linear time algorithm time is. It is for this reason that in management and computation parallelisation of threads that participate in computation or design is performed. The algorithm in Fig.3 is linear with one single path. There are models of nonlinear network algorithms that allow multiple possible computation trajectories [257]. Let us consider one more linear time algorithm This is the algorithm of database query or database search (Fig.4.4)

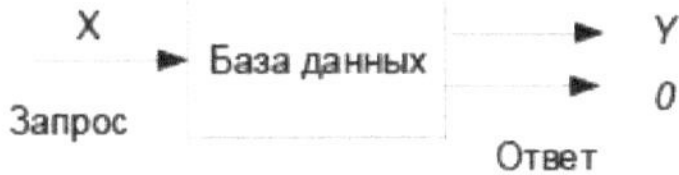


Fig.4.4 Results of the database query algorithm

For Fig. 4.4 the solution condition is 3Y(X) eDB. In complexity theory it is considered that, in general, a decision problem does not always have only two possible outputs, yes or no (or alternately 1 or 0) on any input. Hence, if a solution has only two possible outputs (Fig. 4.4), it is a feature of an algorithm of the first kind. The feature of the algorithm in Fig.4.4 is the unambiguity of the result. It can be obtained "yes" or not obtained "no". At the same time, the result is characterised by the uniqueness of the value Y.

Let us introduce the notion of "algorithm efficiency". The factor of algorithm efficiency is not always evaluated when analysing its complexity. An algorithm can work for a short time and achieve the desired result or goal. An algorithm may run for a long time but achieve nothing. An example of the latter is looping. The efficiency of an algorithm is the comparison or comparative evaluation of the obtained result and the target result. Let's consider the algorithm of a database query (Fig. 4.4). Its efficiency is evaluated quite simply.

$$X_\wedge Ei \rightarrow Y \ (4.1)$$

$$X \cap Ei \rightarrow \varnothing \ (4.2)$$

Expression (4.1) says that the result in the circuit in Fig. 4.4 has been achieved. Based on the query on the input information (X) by comparing it with some database element Ei, the required output information Y is found that meets the information needs of the query. Expression (4.2) says that the result is not achieved. The enumeration of all database elements does not result in information that meets the information needs of the query. The intersection of the input information (X) by the database elements Ei gives an empty set. The second cause of expression (4.2) may be a poor quality algorithm. In this case, expression (4.1) characterises an efficient algorithm, and expression (4.2) characterises an inefficient algorithm.

Expressions (4.1), (4.2) characterise the performance and time complexity. It is linear. For expression (4.1) the running time of the algorithm T1<T(n). For expression (4.2) the running time of the algorithm T2=T(n). In both cases there is a time linear complexity or linear time complexity $O(n)$. Recall that linear complexity is characterised not by the actual running time, but by the asymptotic

value, which does not exceed $O(n)$. In the considered case T1<T2. But both times are commensurable and belong to the same complexity algorithm.

An alternative and qualitatively different database query algorithm is the information array search algorithm Fig. 4.5.

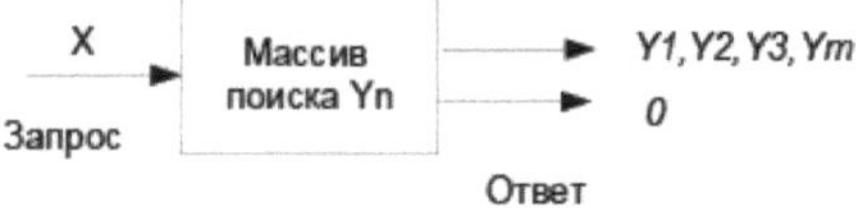


Fig. 4.5. Algorithm of search in the information array

The difference between the algorithm in Fig. 4.5 from the algorithm in Fig. 4.4 in the result, condition and running time. The search result is multiple. The result is not a single value as in the query. but a set of values Ym. The running condition of the algorithm is $X \Leftrightarrow Y$, where $\Leftrightarrow$ symbol denotes qualitative proportionality [258-263]. In both cases, array enumeration takes place. But in the case of database query, the enumeration ends when a match is found with the query. Theoretically, it is possible that the first query produces the required result. In the case of information search, the whole array is always processed.

There are classes and types of complexity. Quite a lot is said about classes and less is said about types of complexity. For the class of polynomial complexity, species are all algorithms that can be described by polynomials $O(1)$, $O(n)$, $O(a(n))$, $O(n \log(n)$, $O(n^a)$ and others. We note some of the algorithms. Inverse Ackerman time $O(a(n))$ - The time per operation using a non-intersecting set. Logarithmic DLOGTIME $O(\log(n))$ time for binary search. Fractional power $O(n^c)$, where 0 < s < 1 - kd - tree search and others.

Complexity classes group computational problems according to their resource requirements. For this purpose, computational problems are distinguished by upper bounds on the maximum amount of resources that the most efficient algorithm requires to solve them. In particular, complexity classes are related to the rate at which the resource requirements for solving a computational problem grow as the size of the input increases. For example, the amount of time required to solve problems in the complexity class P grows relatively slowly as the size of the input increases, whereas it grows relatively quickly for problems in the exponential EXPTIME complexity class (or, more precisely, for problems in EXPTIME that are out of P, since $P \subset$ EXPTIME).

In computational complexity theory, the class P, also known as PTIME or DTIME($n^{O(1)}$), is one of the main complexity classes . It contains all decision problems that can be solved by a deterministic Turing machine using a polynomial amount of computation time or polynomial time. Many algorithms of the first kind have polynomial time complexity (e.g., fast sorting, insertion sorting, binary search)

Many complexity classes are defined using the concept of reduction. Reduction is the transformation of one complex problem into a simple one. It reflects the notion that one problem or algorithm is no less complex than another problem. For example, if problem X can be solved using an algorithm for problem Z, it follows that X is no more complex than Z. In addition to reductions, reductions are applied. There are many different types of complexity comparison based on reduction methods such as: Cook's reduction, Karp's reduction, Levin's reduction. Reduction method involves estimating the complexity of the reductions. Although deterministic and nondeterministic Turing machines are the most commonly used models of computation, many complexity classes are defined in terms of other computational models. A number of classes are defined using probabilistic Turing machines, including the classes BPP , PP , RP and ZPP. A number of classes are defined using interactive proof systems , including the classes IP , MA and AM. A number of classes are defined using logic circuits , including the classes P/poly and their subclasses NC and AC. A number of classes are defined using quantum Turing machines , including the classes BQP and QMA. The study of relations between complexity classes forms the subject of research in computational complexity theory. Regular attempts are made to construct general hierarchies of complexity classes. For example, there is a well-known attempt to relate temporal and spatial complexity classes (in bold) as follows: L

$\subset$ **NL** $\subset$P $\subset$NP $\subset$**PSPACE** $\subset$EXPTIME $\subset$**EXPSPACE**. However, many relations have not yet been explicitly revealed, such as the problem of the relationship between P and NP. Relations between classes often answer questions about the fundamental nature of computation. The relationship between P and NP is directly related to the questions of deterministic and nondeterministic computation. The convention of the division into classes should be noted. The complexity class does not specify the physical computation time. The physical computation time depends on the amount of data being processed. There may be a situation in which a simpler complexity class spends more time on calculations than a more complex one. A shortcoming of the existing theory of algorithmic complexity is the exclusion of the cognitive and cognitive complexity factor from consideration [264,265]. This is the subject of further research. The existing complexity theory [266-269] emphasises on computation and computation time. But the main thing in computation is the result. If the result of computation is not qualitative or fuzzy, the computation time loses its importance. Accordingly, the evaluation of complexity classes should be tied not only to time, but also to the quality of the result. In this connection it is expedient to use the parameter of the efficiency of calculations in the analysis of complexity classes. It is reasonable to use the notion of information units when analysing complexity, giving them the meaning of information units of calculations, information units of time operations. Algorithms of the first kind are algorithms of relatively uncomplicated classes. This makes it possible to study them in more detail, and this paper is one of the stages of such studies.

### 4.1.Complexity of the software

Algorithm is associated with computational complexity. Software complexity is associated with descriptive and structural complexity. A software component is a unit of software executed on one computer within one computational process. Although it is defined as a unit, it is not an information unit, but a composite model [270, 271]. Software can be monolithic (a single module) or it can consist of blocks called components. For software components, the complexity increases due to additional and possibly different relationships between components. Software components are used in complex conditions of changing computational situation or computation conditions.

Complexity theory [272, 273] studies solvable problems and investigates the resources required to solve them. Traditionally, for sequential computations one considers time as a resource, which is reduced to the number of steps of a Turing machine. Another resource is the computation volume, which is reduced to the length of the Turing machine tape. In accordance with this, we distinguish temporal and spatial complexity. In some cases, additional capabilities are added to computational models, such as obtaining random numbers Tasks are classified into complexity classes depending on the resources required. Complexity theory studies these classes and the relations between them.

• Complexity assessment uses comparative and fact-fixing criteria [274, 275]. The following procedures are used to assess complexity.

• Estimate what costs the algorithm requires within the given criteria and parameters (criterion and parametric complexity).

• Compare two algorithms and choose the less complex one (comparative complexity).

• Determine whether it is possible to improve the given algorithm. If yes, it is relatively complex (relative complexity).

• Evaluate the possibility of applying the given algorithm to solve a particular problem (complexity per problem) on a particular machine (computational complexity)

*A computational complexity class is a* set of computational problems that have roughly the same complexity or are commensurate with each other computationally.

*A metric complexity class is a* set of systems or algorithms for tasks that have approximately the same complexity according to a chosen metric, such as the Halstead metric.

*The predicate complexity class is the* set of predicates P(x) that use 0(/(n)) resources, where n is the length of the input data).

*Structural Complexity Class* - The complexity of the structure described by a graph, estimated based on the complexity of the graph

*Time* Complexity *Class - The* complexity of the time resources required to solve the problem.

Turing proved that some problems cannot be solved and it is impossible to create an algorithm to solve them. These are problems of the second kind. The complexity of these problems can be estimated on the basis of comparison.

## 4.2. Computational complexity

Complexity classes [276] are often defined as classes of computational complexity [277], which form a set of computational tasks that have approximately the same complexity or are commensurate with each other computationally. In computational theory, time complexity is a computational complexity that describes the amount of time required for an algorithm to run. Time complexity is usually estimated by counting the number of elementary operations performed by an algorithm, assuming that each elementary operation requires a fixed amount of time to execute. These elementary operations can be thought of as informational computational units. Thus, the amount of time taken and the number of elementary operations performed by an algorithm differ by no more than a constant factor or scale of information units.

The running time of an algorithm is usually denoted by *T(n)*. The time complexity is usually expressed using the big *O* notation, usually *O(n), O (n log(n), O (n^a ) O(2^n )*, etc., where n is the size of the input data in bits 1odd required to represent the input data. Algorithmic complexities are classified according to the type of function denoted by the large notation *O*. For example, an algorithm with time complexity is a *linear time algorithm* and an algorithm with time complexity for some constant *a>1* is an *algorithm with polynomial time.* The concept of polynomial time leads to several classes of time complexity in computational complexity theory. Some important classes defined using polynomial time are summarised in Table 4.1.

Table 4.1. Classes of time complexity

| P | Complexity class of decision-making problems that can be solved on a deterministic Turing machine in polynomial time |
|---|---|
| QP | Complexity class of decision-making problems that can be solved on a deterministic Turing machine in quasi-polynomial time |
| NP | Complexity class of decision-making problems that can be solved on a non-deterministic Turing machine in polynomial time |
| E | The complexity class of decision-making problems that can be solved on a deterministic Turing machine in linear exponential time |
| ZPP | The complexity class of problems that can be solved with zero error on a probabilistic Turing machine in polynomial time |
| RP | Complexity class of decision problems that can be solved with one-sided error on a probabilistic Turing machine in polynomial time |
| BPP | Complexity class of decision problems that can be solved with two-sided error on a probabilistic Turing machine in polynomial time |
| BQP | Complexity class of decision-making problems that can be solved with two-sided error on a quantum Turing machine in polynomial time |

An algorithm is called a constant time algorithm, denoted as *0(1)*, if the value $T(n) = O(1)$ is bounded by a value that is independent of the size of the input data. For example, independently accessing any single element of an array takes constant time, since only one *(1)* independent operation needs to be performed to find it. Similarly, searching for the minimum value in an array sorted in ascending order; it is the first element. However, finding the minimum value in an unordered array is not a constant time operation because scanning each element in the array is needed to determine the minimum value. Hence, it is a linear time operation that takes $O(n)$ time. However, if the number of elements is known in advance and does not change, we can say that such an algorithm is a constant-time operation

Despite the name "constant time", the runtime need not be independent of the array size, but the upper bound on the runtime must be bounded regardless of the array size. For example, the task "exchange the values of $a$ and $b$ if $a \leq b$ " is called constant time, even though the time may depend on whether $a \leq b$ is already true. However, there exists some constant $t$ such that the required time is always less than $t$.

An algorithm has logarithmic running time when $T(n) = O(\log n)$. Since *log a and log bn* are related by a constant multiplier, such a multiplier is irrelevant to the classification of large *O*, the standard use of logarithmic running time algorithms *is O log n )* regardless of the base of the logarithm appearing in the expression *T*

The algorithm runs in polylogarithmic time if its time $T(n) = O(logn)^k$ for some constant k.

An algorithm has linear time or time $T(n) = O(n)$ if its time complexity is $O(n)$. This means that the running time increases at most linearly with the size of the input. More precisely, it means that there exists a constant $c$ such that the running time does not exceed $cn$ for each input of size $n$. For example, a procedure that adds all elements of a list takes time proportional to the length of the list if the addition time is constant or at least bounded by the constant

An algorithm is called polynomially complex (P, Table 4.1) if its duration will be bounded from above by a polynomial expression in the dimensions of the input data for the algorithm, i.e., $T(n) = O(n^k)$ for some positive constant k [278]. Problems for which there exists a deterministic algorithm with polynomial time belong to the complexity class P, which is central to the field of computational complexity theory . Cobham's thesis states that polynomial time is synonymous with the words "obedient" *tractable, "feasible" feasible,* "efficient" or "fast" [279].

The algorithm for sorting $n$ integers performs $Ap^2$ operations for some constant A. Thus, it runs in time $On^2$ and is an algorithm with polynomial time. All basic arithmetic operations (addition, subtraction, multiplication, division and comparison) can be performed in polynomial time. Maximum pairwise combinations in graphs can be found in polynomial time.

In some contexts, especially in optimisation, one distinguishes between algorithms with strictly polynomial and weakly polynomial time. These two concepts are only relevant if the input data of the algorithms consist of integers. Strongly polynomial time is defined in the arithmetic model of computation. In this model of computation, basic arithmetic operations (addition, subtraction, multiplication, division and comparison) are performed in a single time step, regardless of operand sizes. An algorithm runs in strongly polynomial time if the number of operations in the arithmetic model of computation is bounded by a polynomial of the number of integers in the input instance; and also the space used by the algorithm is bounded by a polynomial of the size of the input data.

Any algorithm with these two properties can be converted into an algorithm with polynomial time by replacing arithmetic operations with suitable algorithms for performing arithmetic operations on a Turing machine (MT).

An algorithm that executes in polynomial time but is not strongly polynomial is called weakly polynomial [280]. A well-known example of a problem for which an algorithm with weakly polynomial time is known, but is not known to admit an algorithm with strongly polynomial time, is linear programming. Weakly polynomial time should not be confused with pseudo-polynomial time

Class P is the smallest class of time complexity on a deterministic machine that is robust to changes in the machine model. For example, going from one Turing machine to a multi-machine Turing machine may result in a quadratic speedup, but any algorithm that runs in polynomial time under one model also does so on another. Any tasks on an abstract machine can have a complexity class corresponding to the tasks that can be solved on that machine in polynomial time

*NP class.* The class NP (Non-deterministic polynomial) is a set of problems whose solution is possible given some additional information (the so-called solution certificate), i.e. the possibility to "quickly" (in time not exceeding a polynomial of the data size) check the solution on a Turing machine. Equivalently, the class NP can be defined as the set of problems that can be "quickly" solved on a nondeterministic Turing machine.

It is believed that it is much more difficult to estimate the complexity of a problem than to check the correctness of the solution. The class of problems whose solution can be verified in polynomial time is denoted NP.

$p{:}N \to N$ A language $L \subset \{0,1\}^*$ is said to belong to class NP if there exists a polynomial polynomial-time Turing machine $M$ such that for all words $x \in \{0,1\}^*$ of length $n$ $x \in L$ if and only if there exists $u \in \{0,1\}^{p(n)} : M(x,u) = 1.$ . The machine $M$ is called verifying if its input, in addition to the input word, is a binary word, called a certificate, which allows to verify that the input word belongs to the considered language in polynomial time. A certificate is a verbal analogue of a benchmark. It contains special information, by which it is possible to establish whether the input word belongs to the given language. Restriction, the length of the certificate should be limited by a polynomial of the input word length

There is an unsolved problem in complexity theory (P and NP) which is the question: do all NP-complete problems have algorithms with polynomial time? All the best known algorithms for NP-complete problems, such as 3SAT and others require exponential time. Indeed, for many natural NP-complete problems, it is assumed that they do not have algorithms with subexponential time.

The term "subexponential time" is used to denote that the running time of some algorithm can grow faster than any polynomial, but still be significantly less than exponential. In this sense, problems that have subexponential time algorithms are somewhat more solvable than those that have only exponential algorithms. The exact definition of "subexponential" is not universally accepted [281].

Many graph problems represented by adjacency matrices are solvable in subexponential time simply because the size of the input data is equal to the square of the number of vertices. This conjecture (for the k-SAT problem) is known as the exponential time hypothesis [282]. Since NP-complete problems are assumed to have no quasi-polynomial time algorithms, some results in the field of approximation algorithms assume that NP-complete problems have no quasi-polynomial time algorithms. For example, results on the incompatibility of the multiple covering problem.

A problem is called subexponentially solvable in time if it can be solved in a runtime whose logarithms become smaller than any given polynomial

An algorithm is called exponential in time if $T(n)$ is bounded from above by the number $2^{poly\,n}$, where $poly(n)$ is some polynomial of $n$. Formally, an algorithm is exponential in time if $T(n)$ is bounded by $O(2^{\pi k})$ for some constant k. Tasks that admit exponential-time algorithms on a deterministic Turing machine form a complexity class known as EXP. Sometimes exponential time is used to denote algorithms that have $T(n) = 2^{O(n)}$, where the exponent of degree is at most a linear function of n. This leads to the complexity class E (Table 1)

There are different types of NP-hard problems.

*NP-hard (NP-complex)* problems are problems to which every NP problem is polynomially reducible.

*An NP-complete task is a* task that is NP-hard and is in the NP class. Also denoted by *NPC*

*NP-complete in the strong sense* - NP-complete problem for which no pseudo-polynomial algorithm exists. Also referred to as *SNPC*

Precise statements

$P \subseteq NP$ ; NP.-complete -complete$\subseteq$ NP; NP.$\subset$ NP- difficult; $P \subset NP \subset EXP$

The notion of time complexity introduced for MT can be extended to other models by means of the Church-Turing thesis in a strong form: any computable function can be computed on a Turing machine with at most polynomial slowdown (i.e. *t* steps of computation can be performed by a Turing machine in at most *n* steps for some constant *c,* depending on the particular way of computation). All complexity classes are in a hierarchical relation: some contain others. However, most inclusions are not known to be strict. Class P, which is the lowest, contains all tasks that can be solved in polynomial time. The class NP contains all problems that can be solved in polynomial time only by a nondeterministic Turing machine (this is a variant of a regular Turing machine that can make assumptions). Such a machine makes an assumption about the solution of the problem "or "lucky guess" by trying all assumptions in parallel - and checks its assumption in polynomial time.

## 5. Information design

Information construction is a process close to algorithmic logic. The diversity of existing and emerging models leads to the necessity of generalising models and creating some models over models that could efficiently perform model construction and analysis. One such generalised model is the information construct [283-285]. The process of constructing an information construct and the process of applying the information construct is called information construction. Information construction is a multidimensional model. It is aimed at describing a particular object, process, phenomenon or other entity [286].

Information constructs have varieties. Logical information constructs [287] are logically expressions that are further transformed into logical schemes and algorithm schemes. Network information constructs represent distributed systems, networks or structures of cyber-physical systems. Algorithmic information constructs are generalised schemes of algorithms oriented to solve a group of problems of the subject area. Analytical information constructs are generalised schemes of problem solving and process descriptions. Procedural information constructs are generalised descriptions of processes oriented on the description of phenomena

Situational information constructs are generalised schemes of information situations oriented to construct situations under specific conditions. Meta-model information constructs are generalised schemes of metamodels [288-291] focused on metamodelling. Heuristic information constructions are generalised schemes of heuristic information processing in the form of rules, oriented towards solving problems of the second kind.

Computational algorithms have logical constructs as a basis and convert input data into output using computational functions. Logical constructs are a particular type of information constructs. Functional schemes are a type of information constructs. Block diagrams of algorithms are realisations of algorithmic information constructions. It follows that the information construct is a generalisation of different approaches of algorithm construction. In this case, the information construct can act in two qualities as a metamodel and as the basis of a particular algorithmic scheme.

The information construct as a model of diversity is presented in Fig. 5.1. It includes descriptions of: properties, processes, structures, semantics. The information construct has its own language of construction, which is based on the use of information units, which are not shown in the figure.

Figure 5.1. Information construct as a secondary model

As a secondary model it is described by expression (5.1).

$$Ob \rightarrow IM \rightarrow IK \ (5.1).$$

Expression (5.1) shows that initially the data about the object are transformed into a model, then the model is transformed into an information construct on the basis of generalisation. The information construct is an abstract secondary model. It is at a higher level of abstraction than the primary model. The primary model is derived directly from collection or measurement. In Fig. 5.1 shows on the right the attributes that characterise the degree of generalisation. Object, process, phenomenon - has actual parameters. When building a model, it does not use all actual parameters, but only the essential ones. This is the first level of generalisation or abstraction, when some parameters are excluded and an information model is built.

When moving to a higher level of abstraction, the actual parameters are replaced by generalised parameters. This can be compared in programming with a standard subroutine, which has no actual parameters, but only formal parameters. However, this is where the comparison with a subroutine ends. An information construct at a higher parametric level of abstraction has a description of structure, principles and concepts. Therefore, an information construct can be considered as a model of a class of models, containing class attributes and generalised characteristics. To summarise, we can state that information design is: an object model, a model of a class of similar models, a model of a higher level of abstraction. One of the main tasks of information design is to describe the structure, concepts and principles.

### 5.1. Information construct as a generalisation

When describing and modelling objects of the world around us, dichotomous relations "simple - complex" [292-294] or "abstract - real" arise [292-294] or "abstract - real". This dichotomy gives a reason to construct complex objects from simple objects on the basis of abstraction or to construct structures of simple objects by decomposition of complex objects. Information construction [295-298] is primarily intended for different descriptions. When describing complex situations, processes, models and objects, one tries to unify and simplify the description. For this purpose, the simplest components or information units are chosen, which have different specialisation: semantic [109], paralinguistic [299], interpretive [300], message units [301], logical [302], educational [303], descriptive [304]. Descriptions in an information field may have a higher or lower level of abstraction. Descriptions in the information field can have formal and factual parameters.

Abstract descriptions in the information field contain mainly formal parameters. They are denoted by the term information constructs. Information construction is a concept that generalises information models, information objects, sets of information units, models of information systems, information messages. Information construct is a concept that combines information flow models and models of complex systems. Figure 5.2 shows the relation of information design to the concepts "model", "metamodel", "concept", "idea", "project", "implementation". Fig. 5.2 shows that idea and concept serve as the basis for building an information construct (IC). As such, an information construct can be regarded as a conceptual model.

Information construct (IC) serves as a basis for building an information model (IM) by replacing formal parameters with actual ones. There is a general-private relationship between IC and IM [305]. The information technological design serves as a basis for constructing technological solutions by replacing formal parameters with actual ones.

Fig.5.2. Relation of the information construct to the objects of the information field.

In the information field there is a concept of metamodel. There is an equivalence relation between metamodel and IR. The difference between IR and metamodel is that IR serves as a basis for building a variety of information models on the basis of the "general-private" relation. One of the main functions of IR is to describe and build information models. The metamodel is built on the basis of generalisation of models or on the basis of abstraction. That is, the flows between IR and IM and between IM and metamodel have opposite directions.

The difference between IR and metamodel is also that IR uses information units like in IM. A metamodel uses information units, but in addition to them may use meta-units, which are generalisations of information units.

Information design often has a structure. Elements of the IC structure can be: information models, information objects, information units and heterogeneous aggregates of all of the above.

Information constructs can be crisp and fuzzy. This depends on the conditions of their construction and the types of parameters they contain

Uses. For example, cognitive map and fuzzy cognitive map can be considered as examples of information constructs.

Information constructions as generalisation of information models perform the following main functions: accumulation of experience, generalisation of properties, generalisation of application. The function of generalisation of properties of an information construct consists in that the information construct accumulates experience of description and construction of models and modelling objects. The function of generalisation of information design application is that the information design accumulates the experience of applying models and problems solved with their help. Information construct as a generalisation is a means of describing the picture of the world [306-309].

In the aspect of reflecting the properties of reality objects and their models there are: substantive procedural attributive and combined properties. Accordingly, information constructions can belong to these categories. Substantional information constructs characterise entities, procedural information constructs describe processes, and attributive information constructs describe properties. Fig. 5.3 shows a scheme linking an information construct with its generators, different models.

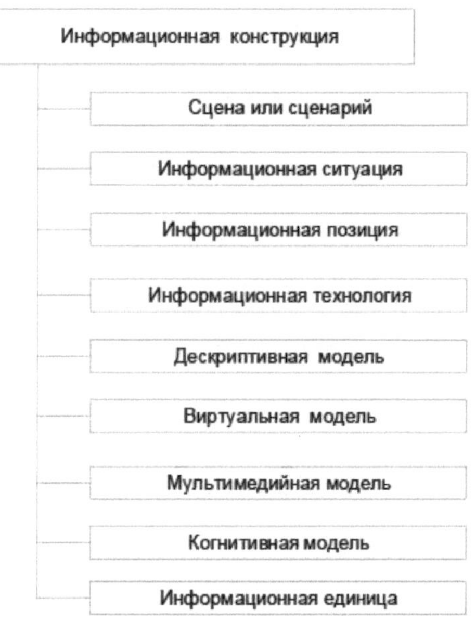


Fig.5.3 Relationship of information design to models.

## 5.2. Technological constructions in the information field

Fig. 5.4 shows the scheme of information technology design (ITD). Comparison of Fig. 5.2 and Fig. 5.4 gives grounds to assert that STC is a special case of IC with emphasis on technological solution. STC is used when the complexity of technologies is high and to describe a complex technology it is necessary to introduce an additional level of description that simplifies the description of technological solutions and increases the reliability of analysing technological solutions.

Figure 5.4. Schematic diagram of the information technology design

ITC is used when the complexity of not only technologies but also technological solutions is also high. In order to describe a complex technological solution in the first place, the concept of ITC is introduced. The additional level of description of the technological solution increases the possibility of its detailed analysis and increases the reliability of the technological solution.

Information Technology Design is a special case of IR with a lower level of abstraction and with a focus on the description of a complex technological solution. ITC does not replace models, but allows to form process models and technology models with greater detail. The level of abstraction of ITC is reduced due to the inclusion of technological parameters, links and relations. The main purpose of ITC creation is to increase the reliability of technological solutions, for example, in programming.

An important feature of ITCs is their adaptability, i.e. a technological solution based on an ITC can be replaced by a new one. A set of ITCs creates a collection of information technology solutions adaptable to specific tasks. The basis for the development of ITC is a conceptual solution, which is supplemented by requirements to the technological solution and to the task at hand. An important advantage of an ITC is the possibility of using a virtual environment [34, 35] or a virtual environment to analyse the ITC.

A number of typical problems arise in the design of an ITS, such as life cycle assessment. ITS has a longer life cycle than technology. It is adaptable to both innovation and application. Adaptation of ITS is most often based on incremental modelling. When solving many typical tasks, their architectural sets are used rather than individual ITCs. The use of an architectural set of ITC reduces the labour intensity of new ITC development and shifts the centre of gravity of work from creation to adaptation. The use of an architectural set of ITCs makes it necessary to integrate ITCs included in the architectural set.

Integration of ITS into the architectural suite is carried out using a systematic approach. Complementarity [310] of ITSs in the set is carried out by means of coordination: logical analysis and comparative analysis.

ITC creates a technological solution (TS), which has an impact on some object A. We will use the following notations: $\rightarrow$ - following or implication; $\Delta$ - change; $\Rightarrow$ - impact. In the expression (5.1-5.3) the models of transformation and impact are given.

$$ИТК \rightarrow TP \Rightarrow A \quad (5.1)$$

$$(TP \Rightarrow A) \rightarrow \Delta St(A) \quad (5.2)$$

Expression (5.1) says that ITC produces a technical solution that affects object A. Expression (5.2) says that the impact on object A leads to a change in its state. It should be borne in mind that

$$ИТК \neq TP \quad (5.3)$$

The information construct model is becoming a common means of conceptualising and describing phenomena in many fields. It describes processes and entities. The information technology design model is a synthesis of IR and technological solutions. The ITC makes it possible to obtain generalised technological solutions. The model of information technological design allows for deeper investigation of information impacts and information interactions in the information field. ITC architectures create a universal mass toolkit for obtaining technological solutions. At the same time, they help in obtaining an estimate of morphological and semantic complexity of the phenomena of the surrounding world. Information technological constructions are the basis for cognition of the surrounding world. The term "information technological constructions" harmonises the semantic field of concepts and terminological relations. The term "information technological construction" fits well into the field of semantic theory of information and contributes to its development.

## 5.3. Constructing an algorithm using logical and informational constructs

Algorithmisation using IR is based on the generalisation of experience in the formation and application of algorithms and the construction of better algorithms on this basis. There are three directions of construction: construction of algorithms for independent solution of computational problems; construction of algorithms for support of information systems; construction of self-developing algorithms. Within the framework of category theory, an algorithm can be considered as a morphism. And information construction as a functor.

Control algorithms have semantic (heuristic) and logical constructs as a basis and transform input decision conditions into a set of alternatives on the basis of analytical and computational functions.

Interpretive algorithms have as a basis the revealed regularities of the surrounding world or information field and transform objective regularities into sets of algorithmic constructions or paradigms. A paradigm is an interpretation and is an example of generalisation of an algorithm. it can be considered as a simple information construct.

The semantics of control algorithms may differ significantly from the logic of computational algorithms. It includes the issuance of necessary control actions at given moments of time or as a reaction to external events. A control algorithm can remain correct with infinite execution under unchanged external situation.

One of the generalisations of the application of algorithms is the solution of the choice problem. The axiom of choice is one of the most important principles of set theory, according to which for any family of non-empty sets there exists a choice function that assigns to each set one of its elements (choosing exactly one element from each set of this family). In category theory this problem is solved by morphism. The axiom of choice is a principle of set theory, according to which for every family of non-empty sets there exists a choice function corresponding to each set by its element.

From this point of view, the algorithm is the principle of choice, according to which for every condition or information situation there exists a transformation function that puts one solution in correspondence to each condition or information situation

Thus, solving the problem of choice with the use of algorithms leads to the concept of information situation as the basis of the condition for the formation of an algorithm and the basis of the conditions for its functioning.

### 5.4. Information algorithmic situation

The information situation model emerged as a need to solve dynamic control problems [311, 312]. Currently, information modelling is widely used in management. The basis of information modelling is an information model. According to [313], an information model is a purposeful formalised representation of an existing object or system by means of a system of interrelated, identifiable, informatively defined parameters. The development of management methods and management situations entails the need to introduce new information models that improve the quality of management. Such models include models of information situation and information position.

In the aspect of management, situational management is developing among

different schools of management. The joint development of ideas of these directions leads to the concept of information situation as a new information model. In the development of the concept [313] the model of information situation or information situation is a purposeful formalised representation of the existing situation, in which the object or research system is located, with the help of a system of interrelated, identifiable, informatively defined parameters
The peculiarity of the information situation is that its construction uses the description and content of the microenvironment, which includes the object under study (Fig. 5.5). Fig.5.5 shows an enlarged model of the information situation. The main thing in depicting this model is the possibility of comparison with the model of information construction in Fig.5.2.

Figure 5.5. Information situation model

The model of an information situation is not an object model, but a multiple model. It is aimed not at describing a single object, process, phenomenon or other entity, but at describing the interaction of objects [314] in a certain microenvironment. An information situation is a primary model, i.e. it is at a lower level of abstraction compared to an information construct.
The model of an information situation is not an object model, but a complex model. It is aimed at describing not a separate object, process, phenomenon, but a complex of objects belonging to different classes and different qualities. The model of an information situation is not a class model, but an interclass model. A model of an information situation includes not only a description of a set of objects, but also a description of the microenvironment in which these objects or processes exist. By this feature it is an open model or an open system in comparison with an information construct.
The information situation should be considered a model of the real

microenvironment, reflecting the information interactions of the system (object) under study in this microenvironment. The description of the information situation should include:

- A description of the current goals and objectives being addressed by the system;
- A description of the current information needs of the system;
- A description of the available information resources and the current situation as it relates to the system, including the states and nature of the actions of the system and interacting systems;
- description of the states of information correspondence between the elements of the system;
- description of the state of information interaction and co-operation processes in the system;
- description of the nature and content of external information impacts on the system and internal information impacts on the system elements.

Information situation as well as information construction use information units as a basis for its construction. The application of information situation models improves the quality of management of a particular system. Application of information design models improves the quality of analysis of a particular system and performs interdisciplinary knowledge transfer. Models of information situation and information design are new information models that allow solving new problems. Models of information situation and information design complement each other and allow to solve in-depth the problems of management and analysis and description of the surrounding world.

## 6. Probabilistic logic in algorithm construction

Probabilistic algorithms in information processing, teaching, cognition and testing use probabilistic logic. Probabilistic logic evaluates [60, 63, 70, 75] the truths of statements taking values in the interval ($0<x<1$) [315, 196]. When using probabilistic logic, it is additionally necessary to stipulate which base logic is used in probabilistic logic. If the underlying logic is binary, then two logical values are used: "true", "false". For ternary logic, a third value, "uncertainty", is added to the two values. What is important for probabilistic logic is that it analyses statements. At the same time, the following are not considered to be logical statements: question sentences (complete uncertainty); definitions; undefined expressions about which it is impossible to say unambiguously whether they are true or false. No conclusion can be drawn from a question, just as no conclusion can be drawn from a single premise. Definitions are identically true expressions. Undefined expressions require additional information to determine the domain of existence of a function or logical expression on which the domain of truth can be found. A statement can be viewed as an information unit. As an information unit, an utterance can be simple or compound. It is simple if it does not include other statements.

This is an example of system indivisibility. Sometimes probabilistic logic is considered as a kind of induction. This is because the relation between the units of inductive reasoning can be evaluated by means of probability. The value of a given probability can be quantified quantitatively or qualitatively (more, less, very much, the most). For probabilistic logic, we can introduce the concept of a probabilistic logical unit. A probabilistic logical unit is a simple statement that is characterised by the probability of realisation of this statement.

Probabilistic logic (PL) is related to pragmatic probabilistic logic (PPL). In PVL, the concept of probability is used to analyse pragmatic aspects of research (probabilistic logics of action, probabilistic logics of choice, probabilistic logics of change, probabilistic logics of preference, probabilistic logics of evaluation, probabilistic logics of testing).

The goal of probabilistic reasoning is to combine the property of probability theory to handle uncertainty with the ability of deductive logic to utilise the structure of a formal argument . The result is a richer and more expressive formalism with a wide range of possible applications

### 6.1. The evolution of probabilistic logic.

The term "probabilistic logic" was first used in a paper by Nils Nilsson published in 1986, where the truth values of sentences are probabilities [315]. There are many implementations of probabilistic logic. Roughly they can be divided into two different classes. The first class is formed by logics that attempt to do a probabilistic extension of a logical embedding, such as Markov logic networks. The second class are logics that attempt to solve problems of uncertainty and lack of evidence (proof logics).

When using probabilistic logic, the cornerstone is that probability and uncertainty are different entities and cannot be equated. On the basis of this we come to a type of probabilistic logic called evidential logic. In evidential logic, there is a need to distinguish the truth of a statement from the certainty of its truth: thus, uncertainty about the guilt of a suspect is not the same as assigning a numerical probability of committing a crime.

Probabilistic logic takes into account the notion of semantics, which ordinary logic does not consider. The semantic generalisation induces a probabilistic logical embedding which reduces to ordinary logical entailment, where the probabilities of all propositions are either 0 or 1. This generalisation applies to any logical system for which the consistency of a finite set of propositions can be established.

It is quite "logical" that a section of probabilistic logic is "subjective logic". The central concept in the theory of subjective logic [317] is opinions about some propositional variables included in given logical propositions. A binomial opinion refers to a single proposition and is represented as a three-dimensional extension of a single probability value to express different degrees of ignorance about the truth of the proposition.

To compute derived opinions based on the structure of argumentative opinions, the theory proposes appropriate operators for various logical connectives such as, for example, multiplication (AND), multiplication (OR), division (UN-AND) and division (UN-OR) of opinions , as well as conditional deduction ( MP ) and abduction ( MT ) [57].

Fuzzy logic is another example of realisation of probabilistic logic. The approximate reasoning formalism proposed by fuzzy logic can be used to obtain a logic in which models are probability distributions. In such a logic, the question of consistency of available information is strictly related to the question of partial probabilistic binding.

Markov networks belong to the field of probabilistic logic. Markov networks can be viewed as sequences of sequences or logical chains. Markov logic networks implement a form of uncertain inference based on the principle of maximum entropy - the idea that probabilities should be assigned in such a way as to maximise entropy, analogous to the way Markov chains assign probabilities to the transitions of a finite automaton.

Non-axiomatic systems also belong to probabilistic logic. Systems such as Pei

Wang's Non-Axiomatic Reasoning System (NARS) or Ben Goertzel's Probabilistic Logic Networks (PLN) add explicit confidence ranking as well as probability for logical units and propositions. Deduction and induction rules incorporate this uncertainty, thus circumventing difficulties in purely Bayesian approaches to logic (including Markov logic), while avoiding the paradoxes of Dempster-Shafer theory. The PLN implementation attempts to use and generalise algorithms from logic programming to take these extensions into account

The theory of probabilistic reasoning is a branch of probabilistic logic. In probabilistic reasoning theory [318], probabilities are not directly related to logical propositions. Instead, it is assumed that a particular subset W of variables V defines a probability space over the corresponding $\sigma$-algebra . This induces two different probability measures with respect to W V , which are called support degree and probability degree, respectively. Degrees of support can be viewed as non-additive probabilities of provability , which generalise the notions of ordinary logical consequence V and classical posterior probabilities for V = W.

This section shows in principle the application of PL in different directions and, accordingly, its importance for practical reasoning and algorithm construction. Let us briefly list the fields of application of probabilistic logic: argumentation theory; artificial intelligence; natural general intelligence; bioinformatics; formal epistemology; game theory; philosophy of science; psychology; statistics; pattern recognition and others. All of the above areas contain cognitive information and are relevant to the research of this paper.

### 6.2. Probabilistic testing.

Probabilistic testing uses algorithmic logic for qualitative and comparative analyses. It is possible to introduce the concept of logical situation and logical unit [319], which expands the field of study and the possibilities of analysis. A logical situation can be analysed independently and together with a group of logical situations, which has implications for education and for testing. The method of group or granular analysis of logical situations allows to reduce unit evaluations of complex logical structures to a set of group evaluations. To some extent, this methodology relies on the theory of ergodic systems and ergodic information processing.

Ergodicity is a property of dynamical systems, which consists in the fact that in the process of development each state passes near any other state of the system with a certain probability. A system in which phase averages coincide with time averages is called ergodic.

Recall that, given sufficient observation time or sufficient statistics, ergodic systems can be described by statistical methods. Preliminary it is necessary to prove ergodicity of the given system. The condition of ergodic processes is that one instance of a process on an interval is equivalent to the whole ensemble of realisations of the process. Information processing processes in information systems are ergodic. Testing processes in education are ergodic. This gives grounds to evaluate them statistically.

For example, the level of preparedness of a group is a measure of the average performance of that group. For ergodic systems, the mathematical expectation over time series coincides with the mathematical expectation over spatial series. To calculate the parameters of an ergodic system, one can either observe the behaviour of one of its elements for a long time, or one can consider all its elements (or quite a lot of elements) in a very short time. In both cases, the same results will be obtained if the system has the ergodicity property. Such systems are study groups.

Testing algorithms often use probabilistic logic. By virtue of tradition one speaks about statistical evaluation in testing. The second reason for not using probabilistic logic in education and in processing educational information is the widespread ignorance of the theory of probabilistic logic among educators. This does not apply to members of Dissertation Councils. Depending on the aspect of consideration it is possible to give different gradation of testing methods.

**According to the type of activity,** a distinction is made between passive, semi-active and active testing. According to the principle of test organisation there are normative testing and free testing. In the sphere of education, most tests are normative. Taking a normative test involves analysing the task and then searching for an answer to a normative question. Such testing is reduced to information search of normative answers in reference books and textbooks. It excludes the creative process. But such testing reduces the information load on the teacher. With such testing, a chemistry teacher can accept testing in physics. A municipal official (who has no education) can test in biology and so on. The testing teacher has the answers to the questions. He does not understand the meaning of the answers, but he can read. The presence of a coincidence between the student's answer and the normative answer gives a positive assessment. In essence, such testing is formally comparative, since the grade is given on the basis of a formal match between the question and the answer. The match is provided by a specialist, while a non-expert uses the knowledge of a specialist. There are also complex methods of assessing learning outcomes that include different testing methods.

## 6.3. Individual and group testing

Ergodic testing and processing [320-323] actually uses probabilistic logic and the assumption of an ergodic component of knowledge. This assumes groups of students with approximately equal abilities to perceive, analyse and reproduce knowledge within a group and differences in these indicators for different groups.

Testing is usually carried out using the question-and-answer method. Testing can be conducted in two modes: self-monitoring and examination. The difference between them is that in self-monitoring, the learner is shown the correct answer to a question if he/she makes a mistake in answering it. In an exam, the correct answer is not shown. The question and answer choices may contain text and a graphic (either together or only one of them). The picture may be static or animated. In addition, oppositional variables are often used in testing. Oppositional variables are essentially logical variables that have two values "true"/"false". Sometimes oppositional analysis is combined with correlational analysis, which provides additional information about the test result. Test questions can be of three types:

Single-option question - there are several answer options, of which only one can be correct;

Multivariate question - there are several answer options, of which there may be several or even all correct answers;

open-ended question - the learner must enter the answer from the keyboard (convenient for entering numerical answers; for example, for the question "What is the variance of a constant?", the answer is 0 - the learner must enter it himself, not choose from a list of options).

The test is usually not graded. The number of questions asked, the number of correct answers and the time taken to complete the test are recorded. Based on these data, the teacher gives a grade. In many countries and in Russia [202], the one-parameter (1PL) Rasch model is used to assess the learner's level of preparedness and the difficulty of tasks.

$$\Pr\{X = 1 \mid \beta, b\} = \frac{e^{\beta - b}}{1 + e^{\beta - b}} \qquad (1)$$

In expression (6.1), $b$ and $\beta$ are independent variables for the first and second functions, respectively; $X$- *is a* dichotomous variable taking the value 0 or 1. In many variants, the symbol $\theta$ is used instead of b.

There are two parameters in this model: $b$ $(\theta)$ is the difficulty level and $\beta$ is the knowledge level when answering the test. The variable can be any value [203] $\theta$ or $\beta$. In this case, the other is considered as a constant. In the first case, the probability of correctly completing the jth task of the test $Pj$ is an increasing function of the variable. The higher the level of knowledge of the test taker, the higher the probability of correct fulfilment of the *j-th* test task. Fig. 6.1 shows the characteristic curve of *the jth* test item, showing the relationship between the values of the independent variable 0 and the values of $P_j$.

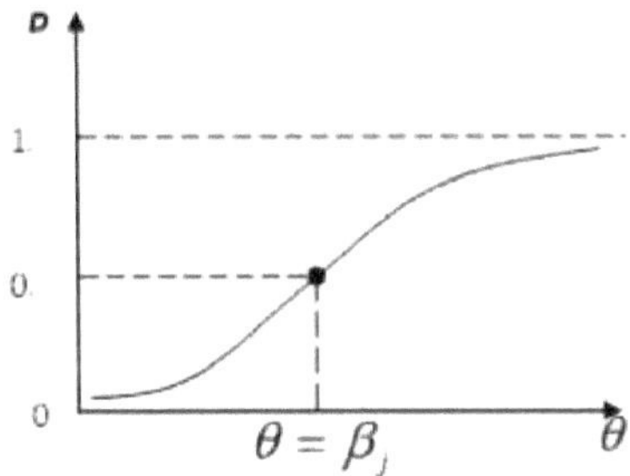

Fig.6.1 Characteristic curve of j-ro testing group.

The inflection point of the characteristic curve corresponds to the value $\theta=\beta_j$, and *Pj* at this point is equal to *0.5*. Thus, a test taker with a knowledge level equal to the difficulty of the *j-th* test task will answer it correctly with a probability of *0.5*. For examinees with knowledge levels much greater than $\beta_j$ -*th, the* probability of a correct answer tends to one. If the value 0 is located far enough from the value $\theta=\beta_j$ and to the left of the inflection point, the probability of correct fulfilment of the *j-th* test task will tend to zero.

Increasing the difficulty of the *j-th* test task by a constant *c (c > 0)* will cause the characteristic curve to shift to the right. With the same probability the test taker with the level of knowledge $\theta + c$. will answer this more difficult task. Since $\theta - \beta = (\theta+c) - (\beta -c)$, , the values of the function $P_j(\theta)$ will not change.

The probability that *the i-th* examinee will correctly complete *Pi* tasks of different difficulty is a decreasing function of the variable $\beta$. . This means that as the difficulty of the tasks increases, the probability values will decrease. The graph of the function *Pi* is called the individual curve of the *i-th* examinee (Fig. 6.2). At the inflection point of the curve corresponding to the value of the independent variable $\theta=\beta$, , *the Pi* function takes the value *Pi = 0.5*. In the process of learning, as knowledge is accumulated, the individual curve of a test subject shifts to the right. There is a correlative relationship between knowledge and test difficulty

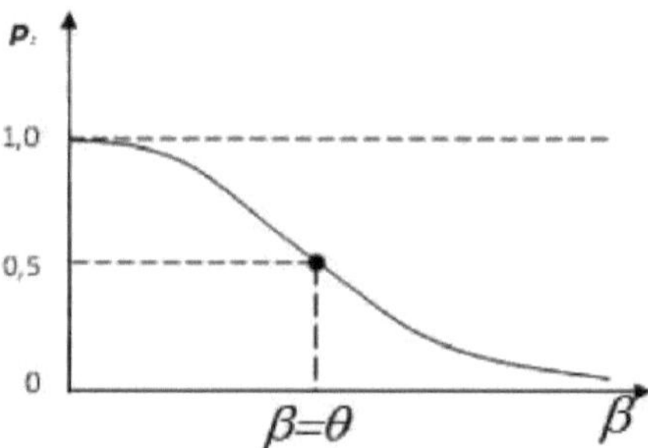

Figure 6.2. Individual curve of i-ro test.

To construct characteristic curves of test items and individual curves of examinees, it is necessary to know the values of parameters 0 and 0. Parameter estimation is carried out under the assumption of normality of distributions of empirical test data both for a set of examinees and for a set of items. The values of latent variables are also assumed to be normally distributed. In the process of test development we have to estimate both parameters: $\theta$ and $\beta$. In the case of using a ready-made test with known stable values of the difficulty parameter expressed in logits, the task is reduced to estimating only the parameter $\theta$. The initial estimate of the knowledge level of the *i-th* test taker in logits is found by the formula

$$\theta^0 i = ln(p_i/q_i) \quad i=1,2,...N \quad (6.2)$$

where *N is the* number of examinees; *pi is the* proportion of correct answers of *the i-th* examinee to all test items; $q_i$- respectively, the proportion of incorrect answers, with *pi = 1 - qi.* Similarly, the initial value of the parameter $P_j^0$ in logits is defined as

$$\beta_j^0 = \ln\frac{q_j}{p_j}, \quad j = 1, 2, \dots, n(3) \quad (6.3)$$

where *n is the* number of items;. *pj is the* share of correct answers of all examinees in the group to the *j-th* test item; *qj is the* share of incorrect answers, with *pj = 1 - cf*

Theoretically the values of parameters 0 and p. can vary in the interval $(-\infty,+\infty)$, т.e $-\infty < \theta < +\infty$ yes and similarly $-\infty < \beta < +\infty$. But practically at $\beta < -6$ *pi* values are close to one *(pi = 0.999...).* Everyone copes with these tasks in the test, and they turn out to be simply superfluous. Equally useless are the tasks at $\beta > 6$. Not a single test taker in the group can cope with these tasks, and they do not provide any information about differences in students' knowledge. The reasoning is similar for $\theta$.

This step of parameter estimation $\theta$ and $\beta$. is considered as the initial one. After its completion, the values of each of the parameters will be expressed on an interval scale, but with different mean values and with different standard deviations. In the second step, the initial values of the logits of knowledge levels and logits of task difficulty are summarised into one interval scale.

The formula for such artificial conversion of $\theta_i^0$ values to $\theta$ contains the idea of destroying the effect of the influence of task difficulty on students' test scores. At this stage, the scores of parameter 0 in logits are calculated by the formula

$$\theta_i = \bar{\beta} + X \theta_i^0 ) \quad i=1,2,\ldots N$$

$$\text{Where } X = (1 + W^2 / 2.89)^{V2}$$

Here $\bar{\beta}$ is the mean value of logits of test items difficulty; $W$ is the standard deviation of the distribution of initial values of the parameter $\beta;$ ; $N$ is the number of examinees. This formula makes it possible to obtain an objective assessment of the knowledge level of each examinee, which does not depend on the difficulty of the tasks included in the test. On the basis of such estimates, it is possible to correctly compare the knowledge levels of examinees who have completed test tasks of different difficulty and even different tests.

A similar artificial technique is used to eliminate the influence of the mean value of the logits of knowledge levels and the standard deviation over the set of initial values of the variable $\theta$ when estimating the parameter $\beta$. . The objective value of the variable $\beta$. i for the *j-th* test task can be found by the formula

$$\theta_i = \bar{\beta} + X \theta_i^0 ) \quad i=1,2,\ldots N$$

$$\text{Где } X = (1 + W^2 / 2.89)^{V2}$$

$\bar{\theta}$ — mean value of logits of knowledge levels; $V$ - standard deviation of the distribution of initial values of the parameter $\theta$ ; $n$ - number of tasks in the test. This formula makes it possible to obtain stable estimates of the parameter $\beta$. , which do not depend on the properties of the sample of examinees. After estimating the values of $\theta$ and $\beta$. in the logit scale, we proceed to the construction of characteristic curves of test items. The analysis of their mutual arrangement allows us to outline the ways of further improvement of the test and to form a system of tasks for objective assessment of knowledge of each test taker in the sample. For this purpose, first of all, unnecessary tasks should be eliminated from the test. If the characteristic curves overlap one another, one of the items should be left and the rest should be removed, as they do not provide anything for the test as a set of working items of increasing difficulty.

Further attention should be paid to those intervals of the axis $\theta$. where there are no characteristic curves. In the test it is necessary to add tasks corresponding in difficulty to the selected intervals on the axis of the latent variable $\theta$. Ideally, characteristic curves should fill more or less evenly almost the whole interval (-6; +6) of the logit scale. And there should be many more tasks of medium difficulty than at the edges of the distribution of values $\beta$. However, this will lead to an unjustified increase in the test length and, ultimately, will make testing ineffective. Therefore, the decision to eliminate unnecessary tasks and add missing ones is not yet final. It can be considered only as a preliminary stage in test creation, reasonable after the initial collection of empirical data, when the number of items in the test is much larger than planned and designed for just such preliminary work.

Further analysis of the test population is needed to make a more informed decision. The same item can be both effective and ineffective in measuring different 0 values. Therefore, there is no single optimal model for selecting items for the test. The proposed modelling makes it possible to minimise the standard error of measurement of this $\theta$ value by selecting tasks for assessment of the given value in a targeted manner.

The one-parameter Rasch model is not sufficient for a complete solution of the problem. This is due to certain restrictions imposed on the steepness of the characteristic curves of tasks within the framework of this model. In particular, it is assumed to be the same for all curves, which, of course, provides a certain simplicity in practical applications of the Rasch model, but at the same time is a disadvantage. This disadvantage is particularly noticeable when one has to favour one of equal difficulty. If the analysis is carried out without the involvement of a two-parameter model, it is easy to come to the wrong decision and significantly reduce the reliability and validity of the test by removing tasks with steeper characteristic curves and leaving those with flatter ones.

Also, the answer times for each question are taken into account when summarising the results. As the answer time increases, the score decreases. The scoring of each question is calculated using the formula:

$$K_\alpha^i = 1 - (to - tmax)/100$$

$$\text{If } K_\alpha^{i} > 1 \text{ , то } K_h^i = 1$$

$$\text{If } K_\alpha^i < 1 \text{, то } K_i^i = 0$$

where: $K_\alpha^i$ - score of the current question; $K_\alpha^i \in \{0, 1\}$; to - time to answer the question;

tmax is the maximum time during which no grade reduction occurs. The tmax time is set to allow the learner to read the question and answer choices and select the correct answer. It defaults to 15 seconds, but can be adjusted at the instructor's discretion. A score of $K_\alpha^i$ is calculated for each question.

After the test, the overall learning coefficient of the material is calculated (actually it is the coefficient $K_a$ ) according to the formula:

$$K_\alpha = \frac{\sum_{i=1}^{n} K_\alpha^i}{n},$$

where n is the number of questions asked.

As a result, the resulting value of $K_a$ may differ from the value obtained by dividing the number of correct answers by the total number of questions asked if the learner took a long time to think about answering the questions. This is to account for the possibility that the learner may not answer the questions independently: the learner may spend a long time looking up the answer in the textbook and still end up with a low score even if he or she answered all the questions correctly. On the other hand, if he/she did not use the prompts but spent a long time thinking about the answers, it means that he/she has not learnt the theory well enough, and as a result, even if the answers are correct, the grade will be lowered. Each question is linked to a theoretical topic. After the test, a learning rate for each topic is determined by the question scores. Topics with a learning rate of less than 0.7 are offered to the learner for re-study.

Probabilistic logicians attempt to find a natural extension of traditional logical truth tables: instead, the results they define are inferred using probabilistic expressions. The difficulty with probabilistic logics is that they tend to multiply the computational complexities of their probabilistic and logical components. Other difficulties include the possibility of inconsistent results.

The Rasch model is a model in the field of probabilistic logic. The one-parameter Rasch model is the simplest in Item Response Theory [188]. Methodologically, this theory of testing is based on the existence of ergodic information interaction between the test and the learner. Different methods of test evaluation can be used for information interaction, including the systematic approach [324]. The main idea of the logit method is to justify the correlation between the answers of students of the same group and the same stream in learning the knowledge of the studied subject. It is assumed that answers to tests are not random, but correlated with the general level of knowledge. The second correlation is considered to be the dependence of test difficulty on the level of preparation. The technological essence of the method is that the answers of a set of examinees to a set of test items are predicted on the basis of mathematical models in the presence of an empirically obtained matrix of initial test scores $X_{ij}$, where index $i$ indicates the number of the examinee and index $j$ indicates the number of the item. Different intervals are allowed for the scores. The idea of scoring is similar to the Rasch model given above in the adaptive testing section. The measure of task difficulty. - are the $ln\ q_j/p$ values corrected during the scaling process. It is this measure that is taken as the final measure of task difficulty. In logit theory, it is called the task difficulty parameter. The $ln\ q_j/p$. value is adjusted to construct a common (unified) scale of task difficulty level and test takers' proficiency level. This is a scaling process [205, 206] conducted using various statistical packages. The adjusted values of $ln\ p_i/q_i$ are called the test taker's preparedness parameter at number $i$. All logistic models can be used to test knowledge or to investigate processes that are described by logistic curves. The simpler the model is, the easier it is to use it in practice, because in this case it is necessary to find a smaller number of parameters. However, for qualitative testing it is necessary to use a larger number of parameters.

## 7. Logical justification
### 7.1.Logical sequences

Logical consequence and logical sequence are different concepts and different models. Logical consistency is a descriptive model. Logical consequence is a prescriptive model. Formal logic has two main tasks: searching for the truth of statements; formation of logical consequence, the semantic notion of which was introduced by Tarski in 1936. Logical consequence is a chain using logical relations existing between premises and conclusions. In an information field, they are described by information relations. The concept of logical consequence does not always allow for a precise definition. In a number of cases its description with the help of modal terms "apparently", "follows" and similar contains an implicit circle, because they are synonyms of the word "follows".

The existence of direct algorithms and algorithms of the first kind was noted above. All computational procedures are carried out on the basis of algorithms of the first kind. Therefore, the analysis of any information processing is reduced to the construction of a complex system of algorithms, which consists of elementary algorithms of the first kind. There is a concept of information units. In the theory of information processing there is every reason to introduce the notion of algorithmic information units. During the transition to logical analysis, algorithmic information units are transformed into simple logical schemes, which serve as a basis for creating complex algorithmic schemes. The principle of creating simple logical schemes and algorithmic information units is the principle of logical succession introduced by Tarski.

The concept of consequence is usually characterised by specifying the relations of one logical concept to another logical concept and, above all, to the concepts of logical regularity and logical model. According to axiomatics, logical consequence excludes indeterminacy, modality, and interrogative propositions. In a narrow, sometimes erroneous, sense, logical consequence is called implication. An implication is a conjunction or logical statement A B that is false only when A is true and B is false. Semantic notion of logical consequence, which was introduced by Tarski in 1936. Formal definition of logical consequence

$$(A1, .... An) \models B$$

Semantic definition of logical consequence: from the premises (A1, ..., Ap) a statement B logically follows if it cannot be the case that the statements A1, ..., Ap are true and the statement B is false (i.e. if B is true in any model in which A1, ..., Ap are true). The distinguishing feature of logical consequence is that it leads from true statements only to true statements. If we consider the implication truth table (Table 7.1), there is only one row corresponding to logical consequence.

Table 7.1. Truth table for implication

| A | B | A→B |
|---|---|---|
| 0 | 0 | 1 |
| 0 | 1 | 1 |
| 1 | 0 | 0 |
| *1* | *1* | *1* |

Logical succession in Table 7.1 is shown in bold italics. All other lines are not logical following. The essence of logical following is the preservation of truth in all cases. This principle is fundamental for algorithm construction.

For the logical succession $\vDash$ there is a close in lettering and meaning symbol $\vdash$ deducibility. The classical logical succession relation $\vDash$ between subsets of the set of formulae $Fm$ and elements of $Fm$ fulfils three conditions FOR all subsets of formulae : $\Gamma, \Delta \subseteq Fm$ и $A, B \in Fm$:

$$A \in \Gamma \Rightarrow \Gamma \vDash A \quad \text{(reflexivity)},$$

$$\Gamma \vDash A \text{ и } \Gamma \subseteq \Delta \Rightarrow \Delta \vDash A, \quad \text{(monotony)},$$

$$\Gamma \vDash A; \Gamma, A \vDash B, \Rightarrow \Gamma \vDash B \quad \text{(transitivity or sectionalisation)}.$$

Different interpretations of the concept of logical consequence lead to different logical systems and to new non-classical directions in logic. Here is an example.

Let $\vDash$ be a relation of logical consequence. Let us call it overdimensional if it satisfies the condition that for any formulas $A$ AND $C$, FROM $A$ AND ***not-A*** follows $c$ (symbolically: $\{A, \neg A\} \vDash B$). Classical logic, intuitionistic logic, Lukasiewicz's multi-valued logics and most other logics are overdimensional. A logic is called parapropositional if and only if its logical consequence relation is not overdimensional.

## 7.2. Analysing stereotypical situations

The construction of an algorithm is preceded by the formulation of the problem in natural language. The transformation of the problem from natural language into formal language can be considered as a transformation algorithm, which belongs to the algorithms of the fifth group.

A problem statement includes conditions, which can be considered as an information situation. Often conditions and situation are described by textual information, which is called content. Therefore, in this case, the construction of an algorithm is associated with the transition from a textual record to a formal logical or functional record. In this formalisation, it is necessary to observe the information correspondence between the logical and functional structure.

Direct algorithms for analysing basic situations are logical schemes drawn up on the basis of natural language in terms of information logical units or elementary logical statements.

Logical and functional structure are related and they allow to create two related schemes: logical and computational. These schemes are logically, informationally and functionally linked if information correspondence is observed. The logical scheme serves as a basis for verification and evaluation of processing logic. Computational (functional) scheme realises the processes of processing and technology of information transformation. Schemes are built on the basis of logical analysis of content (Fig. 7.1).

Fig.7.1. Scheme of algorithm formation.

The initial information situation is always specified implicitly by means of natural language and is a stating or fact-fixing model. Such an information situation can be defined as either fact-finding or fact-fixing. To construct an algorithm, it is necessary to transform such a fact-fixing situation into a formal representation using a programming language or formal logical expressions. The initial information situation can be considered as a staged information situation, which serves as a basis for constructing an algorithm. Such transformation requires linguistic and cognitive analyses. In its turn, the staged information situation should be transformed into a logical situation to check in principle the feasibility of the algorithm and the possibility of its implementation. Fig. 7.2 shows the process of transformation of the initial informational staging situation into a logical situation, which serves as the basis for algorithm construction.

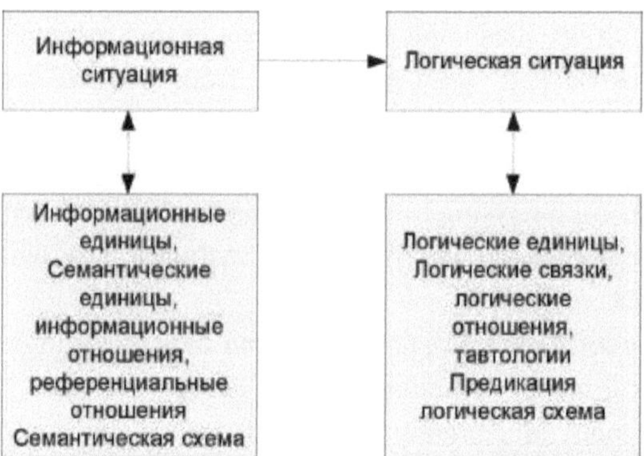


Figure 7.2. Transformation of the initial situation into a logical one.

Figure 7.2 shows that analysing a situation starts with its decomposition as a system or model. Decomposition is reduced to finding information units and relations. And these relations for an information situation should have the form of information relations. In logic there is a notion of a complete system of functions. It is connected with the fact that each formula of the algebra of statements can be matched with a function defining for each fixed set of variables the truth value of the formula. In addition, it is possible to define sets of logical functions with the help of which other logical functions can be expressed.

A system $S= \{f_1, f_2, ., f_n\}$ of logical functions is called complete (or functionally complete) if any logical function is a superposition of functions from this system.

Let $S_1 = \{\&, \vee, \neg\}$, где $\& (x,y) = x\&y$, $\vee(x,y) = x \vee y$ and $x \vee y$ и $\neg(x) = \neg x$. This set consisting of conjunction, disjunction and negation functions is called the standard basis. It is the analogue of basis functions in many parts of mathematics. This set is a complete system of logical functions, since any logical function of statements can be represented by some formula using only the operations of conjunction, disjunction and negation. This follows from the fact that, as noted earlier, any logical function can be specified using a formula, as well as from the described rules of tautologies, for example:

$A \to B \equiv \neg B \to \neg A$ (law of contraposition);

$$A \to B \equiv \neg A \vee B = \neg (A \,\&\, \neg B);$$

$$A - B \equiv (\neg A \vee B) \,\&\, (\neg B \vee A) = (A \,\&\, B) \vee (\neg A \,\&\, \neg B);$$

$$A \oplus B = (A \,\&\, \neg B) \vee (\neg A \,\&\, B);$$

$$A \vee B = \neg A \to B = \neg (\neg A \,\&\, \neg B);$$

$$A \,\&\, B = \neg (A \to \neg B) = \neg (\neg A \vee \neg B).$$

All these expressions are proved using truth tables. These expressions show that some logical operations can be expressed through others. Therefore, information relations are reflections of logical relations. Information units are generalisations and in some cases reflections of logical variables. Decomposition of an information situation into information units and information relations makes it possible to apply logical variables and logical relations to construct a logical situation.

Logical content analysis is based on knowledge extraction methods, inference methods and qualitative reasoning. Qualitative reasoning does not exclude formal description and various formal models. Their peculiarity is the application of formalism without quantitative expressions that require calculations.

Logical analysis is a type of qualitative reasoning. Qualitative reasoning (QR) is an approach for manipulating knowledge that has a qualitative description without resorting to a full quantitative description.

Knowledge representation in qualitative reasoning is carried out through a limited storage of qualitative stereotypes. The transformation of an information situation can be represented as a change of its state. Fig. 7.3 shows such a transformation

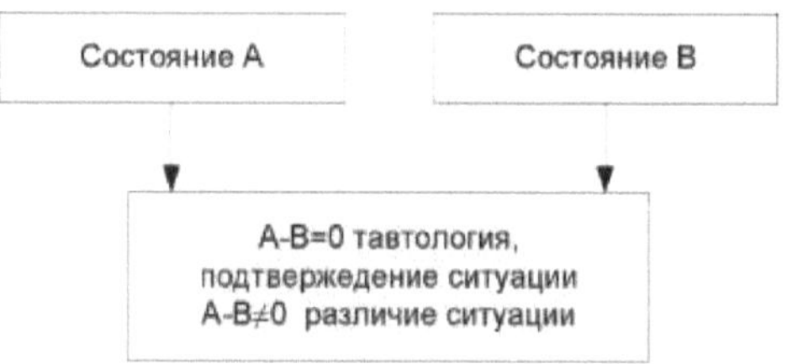


Fig.7.3. Transformation of a situation as a transformation of a state.

In logical interpretation, two states are equivalent if they are tautologies. Tautology in logic is an analogue of information correspondence in information modelling.

In the process of testing and processing information, input and output variables are distinguished. A simple logical consequence between input variables $x$ and output variables $y$ is written not explicitly with the help of implication

$$x \to y, (7.1).$$

Expression (7.1) means a logical relationship between $x$ and $y$. This logical expression is stating, but not constructive. The set of mathematical functions transforming input variables into output variables corresponds to the logical expression (7.1). Constructive is the functional following or functional relationship between input *variablesx* and output variables $y$, which is explicitly written using the function

$$y = f(x), (7.2)$$

Expression (7.2) means the functional relationship between $x$ and $y$. Expression (7.2) has a graphical interpretation, which is shown in Fig. 7.4 in the form of a functional block.

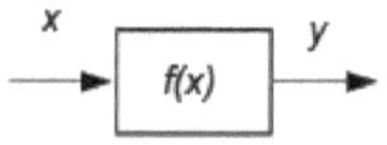

$$x \longrightarrow \boxed{f(x)} \longrightarrow y$$

Figure 7.4. Functional block.

The function box in Fig. 7.4 in systems theory means a black box if the type of function is unknown. If the type of function is known, the diagram in Fig. 7.4 describes a white box. Considering expressions (7.1) and (7.2) together in conjunction with Fig. 7.4 defines functional logical following. Functionally logical following is described by a set of related logical and mathematical expressions describing a common structural composition. Functional logical following can be applied not only to variables but also to functions. If in a decision-making system or information processing system one successively applies a function $f(x)$ and then a function $g(x)$, this can be written by analogy with expressions (7.1) (7.2). The analogue of expression (7.1) will be the logical expression (7.3)

$$f \to g, (7.3)$$

An analogue of expression (7.2) for variables will be expression (7.4) for functions

$$y = g(f(x)). (7.4)$$

If functions $f(x)$ and $g(x)$ are coherent and are subsystems of some system $S(x)$, it gives a reason to write down two system expressions logical (7.5)

$$S = f \wedge g, (7.5)$$

and functional (7.6)

$$S(x) = f(x) + g(x), (7.6)$$

Fig.7.5 gives a graphical reflection of expressions (7.3-7.6)

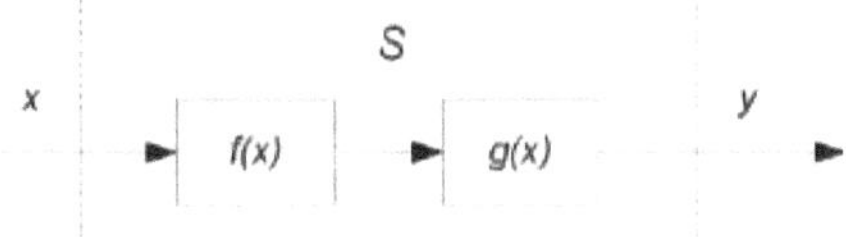

Fig.7.5. The system of functions *f(x)* and *g(x)*.

The set of expressions (7.3-7.6) defines the system functional logical succession. If in Fig. 7.5 we remove the system *S(x)*, then the remaining part and expressions (7.3, 7.4) define the functional logical following.
System functional logical following is a connected description including logical expressions, functions and system expressions describing a single system structure. More complex superpositions of functions are possible. An example of such a superposition is given in expression (7.7).

$$y=h[g_1(f(x), g_2(f(x))] \quad (7.7).$$

Expression (7.7) is structureless, which is characteristic of many functional entries. In practice, one functional expression can have different functional structures. The introduction of logical connectives makes it possible to specify the structure. For example

$$y=h[g_1(f(x), \oplus g_2(f(x))] \quad (7.8).$$

The expression (7.8) corresponds to the alternative scheme in Fig. 7.6

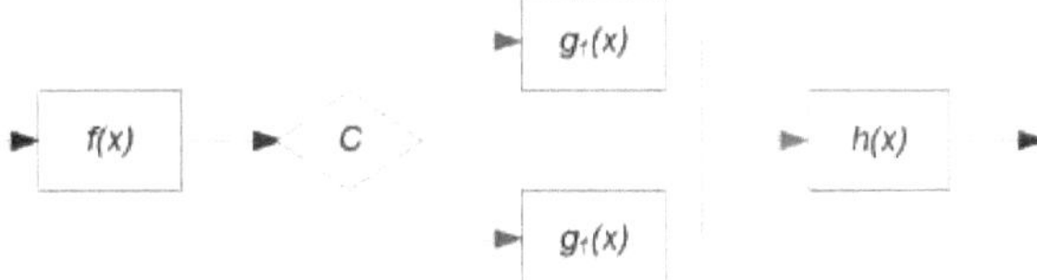

Fig.7.6. Alternative information processing according to expression (7.8)

To realise such a scheme it is necessary to introduce a conditional operator $C=\oplus$, which specifies an alternative and switches the input between the functions upon fulfilment or non-fulfilment of the condition " *C*". This scheme excludes parallel processing of information. Another variant of the structure realisation is possible, which does not specify an alternative, but allows participation of both functions in the process of information processing or calculations

$$y=h[g_1(f(x), \vee g_2(f(x))] \quad (7.9).$$

The expression (7.9) corresponds to the scheme in Fig. 7.7 the difference in the type of operator C= v, which excludes t alternative and admits three possible situations. The scheme in Fig. 7.7 admits three processing alternatives, which are defined by the disjunction property. As such, there is no need for operator C on the block diagram. This scheme allows parallel processing of information.

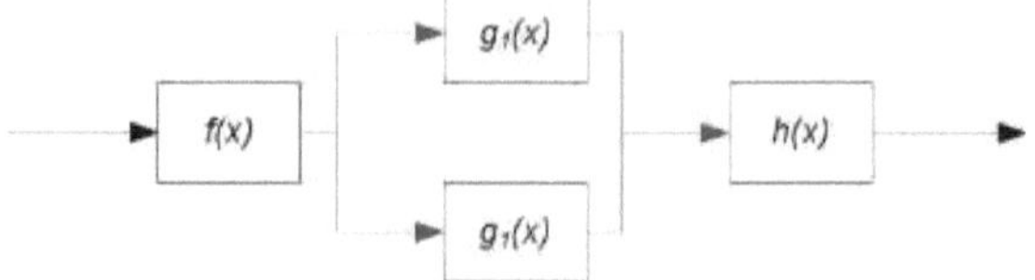


Fig. 7.7 Non-alternative processing according to expression (7.9)

The main purpose of expressions (7.8-7.9) is to determine the structure of the algorithm when processing information. The structureless functional expression (7.7) corresponds to two functional-logical structural schemes (7.8), (7.9). In principle there can be more of them, in this example only two simple schemes are shown. The peculiarity of the schemes in Fig. 7.5-7.6 is that they can describe in a meaningful way real information processing functions or Boolean functions. It is fundamental that a single functional circuit can be described logically or functionally logically. It follows that a real mathematical function can be mapped to a Boolean function reflecting the logic of the mathematical function.

It should be noted that in functional logic diagrams, implication does not correspond to a conditional transition. Although one of the interpretations of implication $A{\to}B$ reads as "If A, then B", the conditional operator is expressed differently in functional-logic schemes. Therefore, it is necessary to reveal the logical description of conditional operators in control and information processing. Fig.7.8 shows a conditional operator acting on the principle of "excluding or" or dilemma.

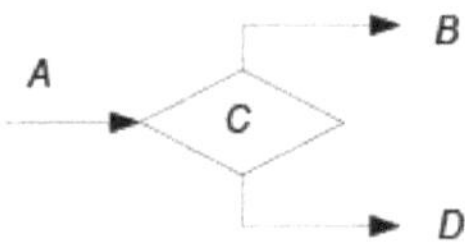


Fig. 7.8. Functional operator of conditional transition.

This operator in logical notation reads as follows: If condition $C$ *is* fulfilled for object $A$, then the transition to process (or object) $B$ *is* performed. If condition $C$ *is* not fulfilled for object $A$, then the transition to process (or object) $D$ *is* performed. The logical check of this transition is performed using the following expressions

$$A \wedge C \to B \quad (7.10)$$

$$A \wedge \overline{C} \rightarrow D \ (7.11)$$

However, in technical systems due to machine failures, it is possible that there is no transition. In this case

$$B \downarrow D \rightarrow A \ (7.12)$$

In expression $(7.12)^{\downarrow}$ is Pierce's arrow. expression (7.12) means that in a deadlock situation there is a return to stage A. To eliminate deadlock situations, ternary logic or a switch with the number of positions from 3 or more is used. This functional diagram is also a variant of implication realisation is shown in Fig. 7.9

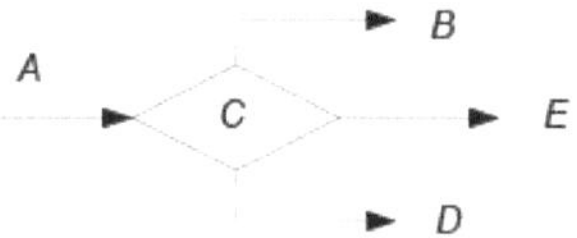


Fig.7.9 Conditional transition operator in ternary fork

The logical description of the transitions in Fig. 7.9 has the form

$$A \wedge C1 \rightarrow B \ (7.13)$$

$$A \wedge C2 \rightarrow D \ (7.14)$$

$$A \wedge C3 \rightarrow E \ (7.15)$$

In expressions (7.13-7.15) $A$ is an input stage with primary information, $C1, C2, C3$ are conditions, fulfilment of each condition entails transition to the corresponding object. In essence, scheme 7.9 means a transition to ternary logic. Thus, it should be stated that in some cases there is no direct correspondence between a logical expression and a functional diagram. A node of the functional diagram and, moreover, an information situation is represented by several logical operators. Figures 7.1-7.9 and expressions 7.1-7.15 can be regarded as algorithmic information units.

### 7.3. Oppositional and dichotomous methods

When constructing algorithmic schemes and decomposing problems, dichotomous and oppositional divisions and corresponding variables are used. Dichotomous analysis develops the logical justification of algorithm construction. Among many methods of analysing logical and algorithmic schemes, two close groups can be distinguished: propositional and dichotomous analyses. Oppositional analysis is based on the use of oppositional variables. Such variables are based on the scheme "yes - no", "object - not object", "relation - opposite relation", "relation - opposite relation", "vector - opposite vector". A special case of oppositional variables are the values of mathematical logic "true-false". Therefore, oppositional analysis is well performed by the methods of mathematical logic. Oppositional analysis uses rigid division and opposition.

Dichotomous analysis is based on the use of a dichotomous qualitative scale and dichotomous variables. Dichotomous analysis is not as rigid as oppositional analysis. Its main axioms of difference and inequality.

Dichotomous variables are used in nominal qualitative scale "object - other object", "colour - other colour", "object - part of object", "one part of object - other part of object", "relation - complementary relation", "relationship - complementary relationship", "covariate vector - countervariate vector", "function - cofunction".

As a rule, connections and relations are used in formalisation. A relation is expressed by the sign of equality = or identical equivalence .                    $\equiv$.

A relation is expressed by a set of logical and mathematical relation operators

$$\approx \neg \oplus \rightarrow \leftrightarrow \wedge \vee \in \subset \sim \neq | \downarrow \notin \vdash \otimes$$

It is the relations that serve as a basis for logical description of situations in dichotomous analysis and obtaining the results of analysis. An algorithm must be logically correct, so it must be created according to the laws of logic and using the language of logic.

Let us consider logical rules for oppositional and dichotomous variables. If $x1$, $x2$ are oppositional variables, then there are logical rules or laws for them that follow from their basic tautologies.

Negation law for opposition variables $x1 = \neg, x2$

The law of identity $x1 = x1$;      $x2 = x2$

$x1 \equiv x1$;            $x2 \equiv x2$

$x1 \wedge 0 \equiv 0$;            $x2 \wedge 0 \equiv 0$;

$x1 \vee 0 \equiv x1$;            $x2 \vee 0 \equiv x2$;

$x1 \wedge 1 \equiv x1$;            $x2 \wedge 1 \equiv x2$;

$x1 \vee 1 \equiv 1$;            $x2 \vee 2 \equiv 1$;

The law of double negation

$\neg(\neg x1) \equiv x1$; $\neg(\neg x2) \equiv x2$;

Law of logical contradiction

$x1 \wedge (\neg x1) \equiv 0$;    $x2 \wedge (\neg x2) \equiv 0$;    $x1 \wedge (x2) \equiv 0$;

The law of the excluded third

$x1 \vee (\neg x1) \equiv 1$; $x2 \vee (\neg x2) \equiv 1$; $x1 \vee (x2) \equiv 1$; $x1 \oplus x2 = 1$

Idempotency of conjunction

x1 ∧ x1 ≡x1 ; x2 ∧ x2 ≡x2 ;

Idempotency of disjunction

x1 ∨x1≡x1 ; x2 ∨x2≡x2 ;

Commutativity of conjunction

x1 ∧ b ≡b∧ x1 ; x2 ∧ a ≡a∧ x2

Commutativity of disjunction

x1 ∨B ≡B∨ x1 ; A ∨x2 ≡x2∨ A ;

Other rules for opposition variables

x1 → x2 = 0; x1 ~ x2 = 0.

Such a large number of rules increases the algorithmic, subject-independent controllability of answers during testing. Their application increases test reliability and reduces software failures. Such a number of rules makes it convenient to create testing algorithms for objective information processing. As a rule, algorithms using oppositional variables exclude the multiplicity of answers and have only one correct answer. The condition of algorithm execution in them is well formalised and unambiguous. The main thing in oppositional algorithmisation is strict checking of pupils' answers with normative answers.

Dichotomous Algorithmisation and Dichotomous Testing is more lenient and allows many conditions. The main condition is distinguishability but not antagonism, which comes from the "law of negation for oppositional variables". Dichotomous variables have their own logical rules that allow for certain logical situations.

If *y1, y2* are dichotomous variables, then there are logical rules for them that follow from their basic tautologies. For dichotomous variables there is a third concept, which we will call some integer (*Int*).

Law of dichotomy for dichotomous variables

$$y1 + y2 = Int$$

Law of difference for dichotomous variables

$$y1 \neq y2$$

Law of Identity

y1 ≡ y1;           y2 ≡ y2

y1∧0 ≡ 0;          y2∧0 ≡ 0;

y1∨0 ≡y1;          y2∨0 ≡y2;

y1∧1 ≡ y1;          y2∧1 ≡ y2;

y1∨ 1 ≡ 1;          y2∨ 2 ≡ 1;

y2⊕y1 ∧ Int ≡ 1

The law of double negation

¬(¬y1) ≡y1; ¬(¬y2) ≡y2;

Law of logical contradiction

y1 ∧ (¬ y1) ≡ 0 ;    y2 ∧ (¬ y2) ≡ 0 ;   y1 ∧ ( y2) - is acceptable;

The law of the excluded third

y1 ∨ (¬ y1) ≡1; y2 ∨ (¬ y2) ≡1; y1 ∨ (y2) ≡ 1;

Idempotency of conjunction

y1 ∧ y1 ≡y1 ; y2 ∧ y2 ≡y2 ;

Idempotency of disjunction

y1 ∨y1≡y1 ; y2 ∨y2≡y2 ;

Commutativity of conjunction

y1 ∧ b ≡b∧ y1 ; y2 ∧ a ≡a∧ y2

Commutativity of disjunction

y1 ∨B ≡B∨ y1 ; A ∨y2 ≡y2∨ A ;

Other rules for dichotomous variables

Y1 ⊕ Y2 = (Y1 ∧¬ Y2) ∨ (¬ Y1 ∧ Y2);

Y1 ∨ Y2 = ¬ Y1 → Y2 = ¬ (¬ Y1 ∧¬ Y2);

Y1 ∧ Y2 = ¬ (Y1→¬ Y2) = ¬ (¬ Y1∨¬ Y2).

These rules derive from the 28 basic tautologies of mathematical logic. The small difference for dichotomous and oppositional variables is due to their qualitative difference.

### 7.4. Hypotheses and corollaries in algorithms

The result of opposition testing is easily verifiable. It is described by a hypothesis from the field of mathematical logic. Recall that in mathematical logic [31] the hypothesis of a formula A means such a formula B that

(B→A)≡ 1.

A hypothesis of formula A is called simple if it is a conjunction of variables or their negations, and after discarding any of its denominators it ceases to be a hypothesis of formula A. Suppose we used 9 oppositional variables x. The student must answer some question prompts positively, e.g. x1, and other question prompts negatively, e.g. -!x6. The hypothesis of the correct answer looks something like this

$$B(x1 \wedge x2 \wedge x3 \wedge x4 \wedge \neg x5 \wedge \neg x6 \wedge \neg x7 \wedge x8 \wedge x9). \quad (7.1)$$

If the learner receives one point for each correct answer, then the sum of the points (Sb) is equal to the sum of the questions (N) under the hypothesis of a correct answer. In a test, a learner may answer a question incorrectly or not answer the question at all. If he/she does not answer one question, for example, x6, then the formula "B" ceases to be a hypothesis and has the following form

$$\overline{B}(x1 \wedge x2 \wedge x3 \wedge x4 \wedge \neg x5 \wedge \neg x7 \wedge x8 \wedge x9) \quad (7.2)$$

The superscript above the symbol "B" shows that it is "not a hypothesis". This is the negation mark allowed in mathematical logic. If a student answers one question incorrectly, for example, x6, the formula "B" ceases to be a hypothesis of the correct answer, becomes a hypothesis of the wrong answer and has the following form

$$B(x1 \wedge x2 \wedge x3 \wedge x4 \wedge \neg x5 \wedge \mathbf{x6} \wedge \neg x7 \wedge x8 \wedge x9). \quad (7.3)$$

In expression (7.3) the wrong answer is highlighted in bold. For expressions (7.2), (7.3) the sum of points (Sb) for correct answers is not equal to the sum of questions (N). FOR THE correct answer hypothesis.

$$N = Sb$$

For the correct answer hypothesis.

$$N \neq Sb$$

In testing, it is not only the result that is important, but also the analysis of the causes that can cause errors when answering a test question incorrectly. To analyse errors in mathematical logic there is a concept of consequence. An error in testing can be considered as a consequence of another error, for example, a wrong set of a symbol. A consequence of a formula P is understood as such a formula C, for which

$$(P \rightarrow C) \equiv 1.$$

A consequence of a formula P is called simple if it is a disjunction of variables or their negations and, after discarding any of its summands, ceases to be a consequence of the formula P. Example of a simple consequence

$$C(z1 \vee z2 \vee z3 \vee z4 \vee \neg z5 \vee \neg z6 \vee \neg z7 \vee z8 \vee z9) \quad (7.4)$$

In expression (7.4), variables z are generalised variables that can be dichotomous or oppositional. Formula (7.4) lists all possible causes of error. If formula (7.1) lists all possible correct answers, then formula (7.4) lists all possible reasons for an erroneous answer. If not all causes are accounted for, then the logical formula "C" is no longer a consequence. For example, the formula CC

$$CC(z1 \lor z2 \lor z3 \lor z4 \lor \neg z5 \lor \neg z6 \lor \neg z7 \lor z9) \ (7.5)$$

He is a consequence because it omits the cause of the possible error z8.

There are general rules for analysing hypotheses and implications that help to analyse in complex situations. For example, any summand of a disjunctive normal form is a hypothesis of that disjunctive normal form (DNF). The summand of a conjunctive normal form is a consequence of that conjunctive normal form (CNF). There are rules.

If A is a hypothesis of formula B, then $A \land C$ is also a hypothesis of formula B.

If P is a consequence of the formula C, then $A \lor C$ is also a consequence of P.

If A and B are hypotheses for formula C, then $A \lor B$ is also a hypothesis for C.

If P and G are corollaries of C, then $P \land G$ is also a corollary of C.

Perfect DNFs and CNFs are often used to solve the problem of reviewing all hypotheses and all implications of a given formula. If A=D, then A has exactly the same hypotheses and implications as D. A perfect DNF has no other hypotheses (not containing letters not included in this DNF) except disjunctions of some of its summands or equivalent expressions. At the same time, a perfect KNF has no other consequence (containing no letters not included in this KNF) except conjunctions of some of its terms or equivalent expressions.

### 7.5. Algorithmisation of statements

In algorithmic support it is important to find information correspondence between logical operators and blocks in the programme. Fig.7.10 shows programme blocks corresponding to logical relations. The blocks reflecting the logical relations of disjunction, conjunction and inversion are shown. The block representation of inversion shows that in programs it often reflects or corresponds to cyclic calculations.

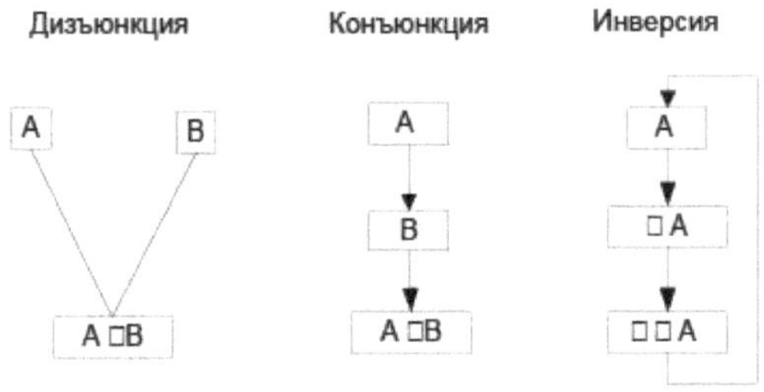

Fig.7.10. Algorithmic representation of logical relations.

Implication or simple logical consequence has the form of a function block

Fig.7.11.

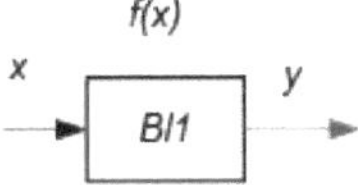

Fig.7.11. Functional implication.

In Fig.7.11 *Bl is the* algorithm block, *x is the* input data, *y is the* output data, *f* is the transformation function. Fig.7.11 can be interpreted using logical and functional expressions.

Logical expression Fig.7.11 $- x \to y$

Functional expression Fig.7.11 $- y = f(x)$

System expression Fig.7.11 $- S: f(x) \to y$

Thus, the circuit in Fig. 7.11 is a linking circuit for logical functional and system expressions.

Fig. 7.12 shows the block expression of the hypothesis in accordance with expression (7.10). In the case of information certainty, all blocks are informationally certain and specify the hypothesis of the correct answer.

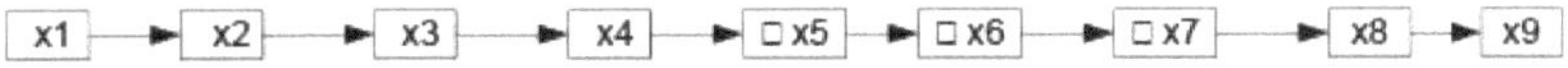

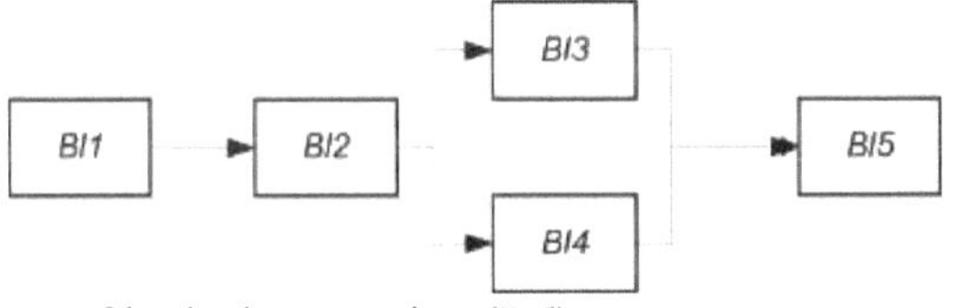

Fig.7.12. Algorithmic expression of the hypothesis

Another important relation must be taken into account in algorithmisation. which does not appear explicitly in mathematical logic. This is the relation of proportionality. Consider the expression

$$(Bl1 \wedge Bl2) \to (Bl3 \vee Bl4) \to Bl5. \quad (7.6)$$

The algorithmic scheme in Fig. 7.13 corresponds to this expression.

Fig.7.13. Structure of logical expression (7.6)

Blocks are related, but between Bl3, B14 there is a relation of proportionality, or Bl3 ®> B14 , or Bl3 " B14. And this relation takes place at the content or semantic level.

When algorithmising testing and test scores, it is necessary to distinguish between connections and relations. The analysis of conditions at the level of textual content should reveal connections and relations, which are then formalised using the language of logic. In order to construct a testing algorithm, all connections and relationships between the blocks of the algorithm must be identified. Depending on the connections and relations that appear, the solution to the problem is broken down into blocks. The simplest partitioning relies on following. For example, it is known that A precedes (B, C, D), D precedes P, H, and block E is the last step in the chain. An approximate structure of such an algorithm is shown in Fig. 7.14.

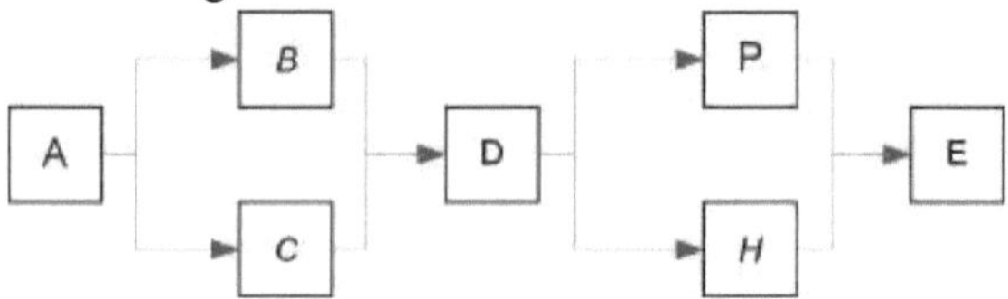

Fig.7.14. Transformation of a logical sequence into a structure

The structure in Fig. 7.14 uses the relations, preceding, last. That is, when algorithmising testing, it is necessary to use not only logical relations, but also a wider class of relations.

Dichotomous and oppositional analyses use relations and connections, which are the basis for analysing the computational situation and information processing. A relation is a mathematical structure [151] that formally defines the properties of various objects and their interrelationships. Common examples of relations in mathematics are equality, divisibility, similarity, similarity, parallelism and many others. The reason for the confusion of relations and relationships is partly embedded in their English terms.

relations connection, relationship,

relationship connection, relation, relationship, relationship, kinship, intercourse

connection links, connection, connection, connection, joining, joining, articulation, affinity

There are relations which are not expressed directly by mathematical and logical operators and therefore they have to be transformed with the help of existing operators, which creates ambiguity of their interpretation, which is determined by the context. Let's enumerate such relations: Proportionality, Integrity, Completeness, Exaggeration, Social, Interpersonal, Implicit, Latent, Heterogeneous, Finite, Similarity, Difference, Oppositional, Antagonistic, Dichotomous, Complementary, Topological, Theoretical-Multiplicity. Most of these relations are complex models that are composed of simple logical units.

A heterogeneous relation is a relation between different sets of

A finite relation is a relation with a finite number of places

Complementary relations - relations of consistency or complementarity and absence of contradiction.

Connection and relation characterise correspondence (property). Strong relatedness characterises a connection $^{\text{connection}}$ - connection, relation, Weak relatedness characterises a relation. $^{\text{relations}}$ connection, relation, For distinction Fig.7.15 and Fig.7.16 show the structures of relatedness and relations.

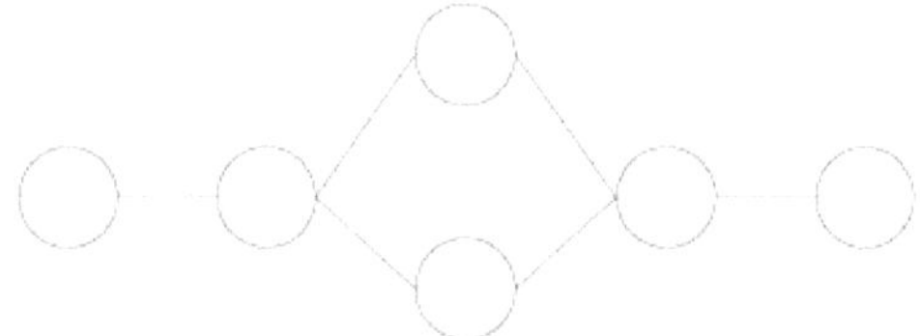

Fig. 7.15 Topological connectivity structure

Fig.7.15 reflects topological connectivity of objects. Fig.7.16 reflects topological relations.

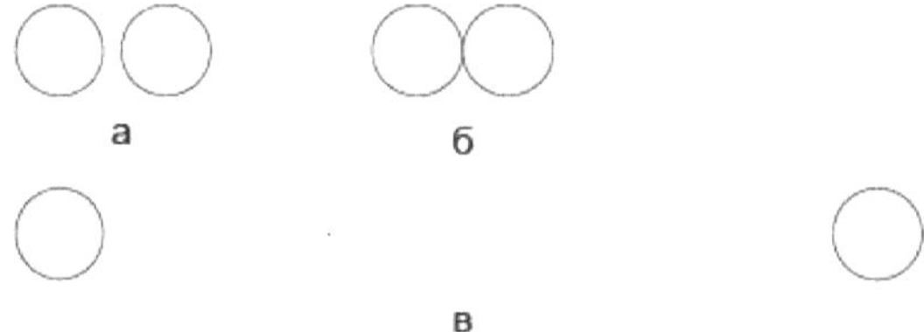


Fig.7.16. Examples of topological relations

Fig.7.16 shows the following topological relations: a - proximity, b - adjacency, c - remoteness

### 7.6. Predicates and quantifiers.

When processing information, it is important to define the truth region (the region of correct answers). In logic, the truth region can be defined by a continuous interval of values. The truth region can be given by a function. Expressions (7.1) and (7.4) for hypothesis and consequence may have a complex form when there are a large number of factors or variables. Quantifiers are used to simplify the analysis and writing of hypotheses and implications. If the predicate P(x) is defined on a finite set $M = \{a_1, \ldots, a_k\}$, then the following identities are true [151]:

$$\forall x P(x) \equiv P(a_1) \wedge \ldots \wedge P(a_k); \ (7.7)$$

$$\exists x P(x) \equiv P(a_1) \vee \ldots \vee P(a_k). \ (7.8)$$

Thus, quantors can be considered as generalisations of logical connectives and compact expressions of the hypothesis (7.7) and corollary (7.8). In the case of predicates defined on infinite sets, the quantum of generality generalises conjunction, and the quantum of existence generalises disjunction. Quantifiers can be hinged on multiset predicates and on any logical expression. The expression on which the quantifier is hinged is called the scope of the quantifier. All occurrences of a variable in this expression are bound. Variables not bound by quantifiers are called free variables.

To a predicate from two variables $P(x, y)$ quantum operations can be applied to one variable or to two variables. Changing the order of the quantors changes the meaning of the statement and its logical value. There are the following tautological statements [31]:

1) $\forall x P(x, y)$; $\forall y P( x, y)$;

2) $\exists x P( x,y)$; $\exists y P( x,y)$;

3) $\forall x \, \exists y \, P(x, y)$; $\forall x \, \forall y \, P(x, y)$;

4) $\exists x \, \forall y \, P(x, y)$; $\exists x \, \exists y \, P(x, y)$;

5) $\forall y \, \forall x P(x, y)$; $\forall y \, \exists xP(x, y)$;

6) $\exists y \, \forall x P(x, y)$; $\exists y \exists x \, P(x, y)$

Oppositional and dichotomous testing complement each other. Oppositional testing is used at the stage of knowledge acquisition. Dichotomous testing is applied at the stage of knowledge consolidation and application. The joint application of these groups of tests gives a greater effect than the application of oppositional tests alone.

Algorithmic information units have graphical equivalents. This gives grounds to translate the problem from natural language into a logical form and then to translate the logical form into the graphical language of algorithm schemes. When choosing methods of analysis, the oppositional approach is preferable as it corresponds closer to mathematical logic and has a large number of logical regularities. Oppositional variables and oppositional expressions can be easily transformed into algorithms of the first kind, which simplifies the performance of calculations. However, in practice, in complex situations one has to use the dichotomous approach when oppositional variables cannot be used. Dichotomous variables and dichotomous information constructions are less often transformed into algorithms of the first kind and more often algorithms of the second kind are built on their basis.

## 8. Spatial algorithmic logic
### 8.1. Peculiarities of spatial logic

Spatial logic [325-330] is a rather broad direction related to spatial analysis and to logical reasoning. In the first direction it relies on qualitative analysis and geometrical logic. In the second direction it is related more to logical formalisation. Spatial logic uses binary and ternary logic. It has to do with fulfilment or violation of the law of exclusion of the third. If there is a spatial situation in which the law of elimination of the third is fulfilled, then the mechanism of binary classical logic is applicable to spatial logic.

Spatial logic is applied in spatial reasoning [331-333]. It has been applied in architecture since pre-Christian times. Spatial logic is applied in landscape design [334]. Spatial logic is applied in spatial knowledge extraction. Spatial logic is applied in chip design and organisation of parallel computing [335]. Spatial logic is used when forming queries to a database [336]. Spatial logic is used in robotics and vision systems [337]. Spatial logic is used in building virtual maps and in augmented reality systems.

Spatial logic is used in interactive information processing in geographic information systems. Spatial logic is used in cartography. Spatial logic is used in geodesy when conducting field work and working with satellite navigation receivers. Spatial logic is used in monitoring of deformations and settlements of structures. Thus, spatial logic is intensively applied in Earth sciences. Spatial logic is a generalised concept and in geoinformatics includes several parts: geometric logic, topological logic, set-theoretic logic, image logic. The area of spatial knowledge acquisition [338-340] is particularly emphasised in geoinformatics, where spatial logic is also applied. Spatial logic is applied in education, both in earth sciences and in other disciplines, geometry topology, set theory. Spatial logic has an outlet in the field of artificial intelligence, where it is applied in intelligent transport systems [341-344] and in transport cyber-physical systems [345-348], digital railway technologies [349, 350].

### 8.2. A systematics of spatial logic.

The main types of spatial logic used in information processing are: geometric logic, topological logic and image logic.

*Geometric logic.* Geometric logic emerged long before the advent of geoinformatics. It includes: axioms; theorems and target statements, which are expressed by means of proof or construction. Geometric logic is applied not only in real space but also in parameter space, for example, when using the method of separating hyperplane when separating two parametric classes. In automated image processing, geometric logic is used to solve problems of spatial object recognition. Geometric logic in this direction is used in unmanned control systems to detect obstacles or recognise objects not visible in the optical range. A distinction is made between geometric logic in the plane and geometric logic of curved space.

The logic of geometry in the plane does not allow parallel lines to intersect. In geometry in the plane, a triangle has a sum of interior angles equal only to l. The logic of geometry on the sphere replaces the notion of a straight line with the notion of a geodesic line. The logic of geometry on the sphere allows the intersection of parallel lines. For example, meridians intersect at the pole, at the same time parallels do not intersect. The logic of geometry on the sphere admits the sum of internal angles of a convex curved triangle equal to 3/2l. Thus, geometrical logic is given not only by basic axioms, but also by the kind of space. This is an essential difference from mathematical logic, in which space is not considered. and postulates and may differ for different geometries.

*Topological logic.* Topological logic is widely used in geoinformatics, in particular in the topologisation of spatial information. Cartographic works use topological logic. When digitising maps based on scanned images, spatial logic is used to eliminate automated vectorisation errors.

In topology, spatial logic uses simple axioms: topological invariance (Fig. 8.1), intersection, absence of intersection. Topological logic uses topological properties of objects, the presence of which means "true", the absence of which means "false".

Figure 8.1. Topological invariants.

There is a relation of logical equivalence between the figures in Fig. 8.1 in accordance with topological logic. They can be considered as logical tautologies. For spatial logic and topological logic there is a notion of topological certainty. It is related to the notion of informational certainty and topological unambiguity This property distinguishes spatial logic from other types of logics. It should be noted that for spatial logic, unlike binary logic, there is a notion of multiplicity of values of spatial images. The elimination of the multiplicity of values of spatial logic is achieved by special conditions and additional notations. This means that the language of spatial logic is extensible and differs for different tasks and classes.

Fig.8.2 shows topologically multivalued and topologically univalued images. The image in Fig. 8.2a is called "spaghetti". It is multivalued and contains information uncertainty.

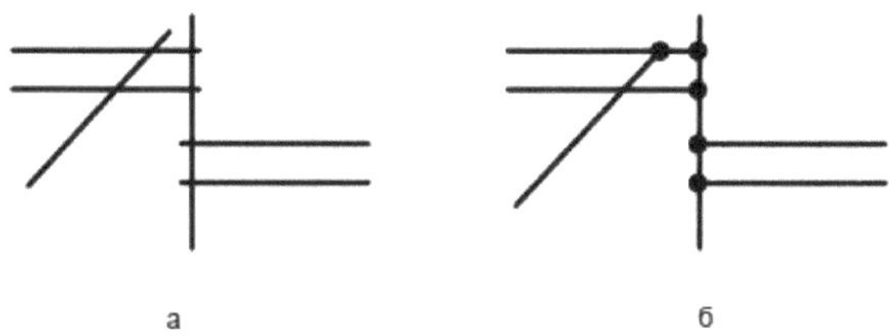


Fig.8.2 Topologically correct b) and topologically incorrect a)
spatial image

The situation shown in Fig.8.2a is typical for automated vectorisation of raster map images. In Fig.8.2a it is not clear: do lines intersect or pass one above another? Is it an error to extend horizontal lines beyond the vertical line? This uncertainty can be a violation of complementarity of real images and a violation of topological information correspondences between the model and the real object. Figure 8.26 characterises the elimination of information uncertainty and the elimination of ambiguity.

To eliminate ambiguity, additional graphic symbols (graphic information units) have been introduced. Point designations have been introduced to indicate intersections. The presence of a point means the presence of an intersection (logical yes) the absence of a point means the absence of an intersection of lines (logical no).

On the basis of additional semantic information (by visual comparison with the map) it was established that the ends of horizontal lines should not extend beyond the boundaries of the vertical line. Correction on this basis was made. Thus, the topological logic in geoinformatics differs from the topological logic in topology by a large number of graphical notations and application of semantic information to eliminate uncertainty and multiplicity of values. The topological model in geoinformatics does not exist independently, but reflects the properties of a spatial object, which are not expressible by means of conventional topology. Therefore, topological logic in geoinformatics is extended in relation to topological models.

In some cases, topological descriptions may correspond to logical expressions. This situation is typical for algorithms. For example, an oriented arc corresponds to implication. Intersection corresponds to conjunction. Topological invariance corresponds to equivalence or tautology. In geoinformatics, a topological model can represent a spatial model such as roads. In geoinformatics, a topological model can represent discrete or continuous flows (logistics) This allows the construction of geoinformatic topological models for analysing the state of transport networks and analysing freight flows. Usually, a topological spatial diagram shows connections.

*Set-theoretic logic.* Theoretical-multiple logic in geoinformatics is also a spatial logic, especially when working with areals and linear objects. At the same time, it uses the formalism of set-theoretic relations, which greatly simplifies the analysis of areal models and checking them for logical correctness of their construction.

Set-theoretic logic uses set-theoretic relations as spatial relations [351] between objects of space and as logical relations by models of objects. Theoretic-multiplicity diagrams display first of all relations, secondly relations. The most striking models illustrating spatial logic are Euler-Wien diagrams.

*Figurative logic.* Figurative logic is the logic of spatial models to which some reality corresponds. Not all figurative models reflect physical objects. For example, the zone of ecological pollution or zones of possible flooding depending on the water level are spatial models, but in reality they may not correspond to a real visible object.

Image logic models include elementary models - information units, which serve as a basis for building complex models and provide an opportunity to compare models, as well as to check their correctness. Correctness of models of figurative logic is first of all determined by correctness of their correspondence to spatial objects. Examples of spatial information units are conventional signs on maps and spatial aggregation language units [352, 353]. Figurative logic is applied in geoinformatics, geodesy and cartography. The most striking sections of image logic are: image processing, interactive information processing in GIS, cartographic logic in map construction.

*Cartographic logic.* Cartographic logic is structurally similar to topology and to geometric logic. A map conveys first of all topological relations and secondly geometrical relations. It is based on certain cartographic rules (axioms) and standardised information units - conventional signs. However, cartographic logic is not yet considered as a section of spatial logic. From 1908 (map logic) [354] to 2010 (cartographic logic) [354] and up to now, map logic is understood only as rules of map construction and map reading, but does not speak about the language of logic. Map logic (but not cartographic logic) is also called [355] the application of ordinary logic to construct and analyse spatial cartographic images. In cartography, the concept of map language has been introduced [356], but in isolation from cartographic logic. Therefore, cartographic logic has not been formed so far as a holistic direction, organically included in spatial logic.

The closest to spatial logic and to cartographic logic is the work of A. A. Lyutoy "the language of maps" [356]. Lyutoy considers the language of maps as a means of systematic description of cartographic works. He considers geographical maps as a systematised set of graphic images and spatial models. He allows creativity in the creation of cartographic composition. But the use of the concept of map language allows us to compare different cartographic situations and to identify a plurality of meanings in map construction. This multiplicity of meanings is characteristic of all spatial logic. It requires identifying the situation and eliminating it if possible. The spatial language of maps makes it possible to analyse, compare and identify multiplicity of meanings or spatial uncertainty.

As early as 1923, Bertrand Russell interpreted the nature of spatial images as a highly informative model: "There is a difficulty about language as a method of representing a system, namely that the words which signify relations are not themselves relations. The graphic image of a map is superior to language because the fact that one place is to the west of another is represented by the fact that the corresponding place on the map is to the left of the other, that is, the actual relation is represented by a spatial relation." [357, c. 152]. This corresponds to modern concepts of spatial logic.

**Errors of spatial logic.** A peculiarity of spatial languages is the plurality of meanings, which can cause inconsistency of interpretation. Plurality in the construction of images leads to logical errors. In his work, Lyutyi singles out only four types of characteristic spatial errors [356]. It should be noted that the noted errors are characteristic both for cartography and for image logic.

To the first type of errors he refers the errors *"figurative similarity-semantic difference"* These errors are caused by the use of figurative signs of different semiotic types, which in the process of composition the same final images. An example is shown in Fig. 8.3 [356].

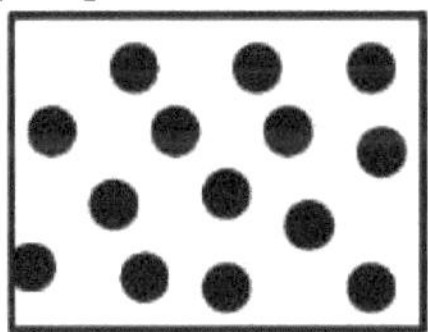

Fig.8.3 Duality of interpretation of the spatial image.

The spatial model in Figure 8.3 can be interpreted in two ways. Each point can represent a separate object or points can represent a property of the areal. The first interpretation of the image in Fig. 3 is a set of point objects on the areal selected by a quadrangle

The second interpretation of the image in Figure 8.3 is an areal on which dots show some property, such as population density or electorate density in an election for some party.

To the second type of spatial logical errors Lyutyi refers errors of incorrect placement of images in the field of cartographic image. These errors lead to appearance of false sign compositions and false spatial relations. Sometimes they lead to the effects of "absorption" of some signs by others. Errors of semantic uncertainty and duplication of information belong to this group. The third group of errors according to A.A. Lyutom is caused by errors in classifications of spatial objects. In the fourth type of errors he attributes errors in the construction of cartographic scales, when due to insufficient number of gradations an important spatial phenomenon is dropped out. The first three types of errors are characteristic of figurative logic in general.

**The language of spatial aggregation as the language of spatial logic.** A section of figurative logic is the logic of artificial intelligence. It is used in automated analysis of parts of spatial objects and their spatial relations. The best known language of such logic is the language of spatial aggregation. It is used in spatial analysis and spatial knowledge acquisition. Figure 8.4 shows information units of the spatial aggregation language [352, 353].

Fig.8.4 Logical units of spatial relations

Fig.8.4 shows the interpretations of the symbols of the spatial aggregation language. Explanation is given from left to right. No interaction - DC. Common boundary interaction - EC. Partial overlap - PO. Tangentially correct interaction TPP. Inverse tangentially correct interaction - TPP*. Object internal does not interact tangentially with object external - NTPP. An object external does not interact tangentially with an object internal - NTPP*. Objects are equivalent - EQ.

The SAL spatial aggregation language allows users to explore spatial relations: neighbourhoods, intersections, equivalences. This language is a typical computer science language. The SAL source set can be downloaded from www.cs.www.cs.purdue.edu/homes/cbk/sal.html.edu/homes/cbk/sal.html or www.parc.com/zhao/sal.htmlwww.parc.com/zhao/sal.html. A broader list of logical units for expressing spatial relations is given in [237]

Tasks in spatial logic are verification, identification, construction, and editing tasks. Pattern logic can be interpreted as any geometric properties of spatial objects or spatial relations defined in different domains: topological connectedness of domains, parallelism of lines or, equally, remoteness of two points from the third.

**Analysis of the state of spatial logic.** In the modern understanding, spatial logic is close to modal logic and temporal logic [358]. A significant contribution to the development of spatial logic by analysing geometry and its logic was made by Tarski [359]. Tarski applied first-order logic with pointwise variables in the plane and with non-logical predicates denoting two primitive spatial relations: the ternary relation "between" and the quaternary relation "equidistance". The language he produced was sufficient to describe Euclidean geometry.

A distinctive feature of modern logic and especially spatial logic is the model approach. It uses different relations between spatial models and objects as a basis. As such, spatial logic allows us to study the relations between geometric images and real spatial objects.

Spatial logic differs from mathematical logic in three main ways. The first concerns qualitatively different sets of geometric objects, which require different logics and different interpretations: points, lines, areas of different kinds, surfaces, volumetric bodies. The second fundamental difference concerns the choice of qualitatively different basic units of description, basic relations and operations on these objects. In this difference, information units are qualitatively different. In mathematical logic they are only formal. And in spatial logic formal and semantic information units are used. The third fundamental difference concerns purely the introduction of uncertainty and modality into logical spatial descriptions. For example, the situation that object A is closer to object B than object B belongs to the field of probabilistic logic and qualitative reasoning.

The basis of transformations in mathematical logic are tautologies and equivalences. Invariance in spatial logic is a complete analogue of equivalence or tautology in mathematical logic. An example is topological invariants. Many invariance relations can correspond exactly to first-order logic.

The main problem of spatial logic is "generalisation - detail" or "simplicity - complexity". Analyses of the complexity of spatial logic models usually focus on two problems: model checking (determining whether a given model is true in the interpretation of the object corresponding to it) and checking whether a given model is computationally feasible. Often, an attempt to represent the spatial model in Figure 7 in words is doomed to failure by cognitive and linguistic factors. That is, this task is intractable.

Most spatial logics above first order, contain contradictions and lead to unsolvable problems of mapping spatial images. An example of solvable logics are spatial logics interpreted by regular topological models. The language of these logics includes only Boolean bundles (without quantifiers), spatial information units (primitives) and represent various topological relations and functions.

Spatial logic even now contains a number of problems that are considered not yet fully understood. The general methodology in logical spatial generalisation is to find expressive spatial models that are logically analysable.

Conventional methods of analysis that deal with simple models are often powerless when confronted with languages interpreted according to specific structures, as is usually the case in spatial logic.

In expressive interpretation, the advantages and effectiveness of spatial logic should be noted. The analysis of patterns of image representation and interpretation is a growing area of research that yields useful applications in areas such as spatial knowledge and visual programming. However, the formal analyses of image representations that have been applied do not always take into account the ways in which spatial relations are utilised in such a representation.

Graphical representations in spatial logic, unlike the apparatus of mathematical logic, have resources for expressing various kinds of real-world uncertainty. The main difference between graphical and linguistic systems is the use of relations. Spatial models use spatial relations to represent the subject domain directly. Linguistic systems use words to represent relations indirectly and can be interpreted differently, depending on the intelligence of the interpreter.

Modern spatial logic is widely used in geoinformatics, but in terms of theory is in a state of development. Spatial logic is heterogeneous and contains special spatial logics. A common concept that can be adopted for all spatial logics is the concept of language. A private spatial logic must have its own logical language. The absence of a language does not give a reason to speak of a logic. An important concept that is applied but poorly described is the concept of information units as logical information units and as the alphabet of a language. Any language has an alphabet, which is formed by its information units. In mathematical logic, such units are logical connectives. In spatial reasoning such language is the language of spatial aggregation. Theoretical-multiple logic in geoinformatics reflects relations and is well suited for working with areal objects. Topological logic in geoinformatics reflects linear objects and is well suited for working with them, including flows. These logics complement each other when working with different geoinformatics objects. The high efficiency of spatial logic lies in the multiplicity of semantic content, while mathematical logic is much poorer. The efficiency of spatial logic lies in the possibility of expressing multiple spatial relations by means of graphics. But it generates a contradiction between its great expressiveness and complexity of its modelling. so far it is solved by attraction of human intellect. In general, this direction is still waiting for its development and theoretical generalisation.

## 8.3.Computational processes

In the modern digitalisation of society and governance, spatial information is important [360]. In this case, geodata are of crucial importance [361]. Coordinates, which determine the position on the earth's surface, are the dominant factor of a property object that affects its market value. When evaluating the efficiency of innovation projects [362-365], the spatial factor affects the diffusion of innovation and needs to be taken into account. When moving material flows, the spatial factor also affects the cost of transport and requires consideration. The dynamics of society development leads to the dynamics of appearance and change of spatial objects. This requires regular collection and updating of spatial information [366, 3671]. A new direction in economics - spatial economics [368], which differs from regional economics and has its own methods and tasks, has appeared and is developing abroad. Despite the intensive development of spatial economics abroad, in Russia this direction is practically a duplication of regional economics.

Spatial information drives the application of spatial modelling [369,   370]   and spatial metamodelling.

An additional challenge is the problem of "big geospatial data" [371-373]. All this makes the processing of spatial information relevant.

*Groups of processing algorithms.* The basis of spatial information processing is algorithms. Algorithms for spatial information processing are divided into direct and heuristic or second kind, and integer coordinates [374]. which are applied in image processing. The difference between direct and heuristic algorithms is. that direct algorithms are implemented on a computer and exclude human involvement in processing. Heuristic algorithms include humans in the information processing. This type of processing is called interactive processing. For heuristic processing, an important factor is the initial information model, which requires preparation. Large amounts of information require interpretation before processing. For this purpose, special interpretation algorithms are used [375]. Interpretation is divided into two groups: pre-interpretation and post-interpretation. Pre-interpretation is required to analyse primary information and to organise it for further algorithmic processing. Post interpretation is required to analyse secondary information obtained after algorithmic processing

The term interpretation covers a wide range of algorithms. The simplest variant of interpretation is associated with the recoding algorithm. Data interpretation technology can be considered as a process by which a data system acquires a new meaning. The algorithm of such interpretation is based on the constructive, logical and functional design that realises the interpretation technology.

There are a number of basic concepts that are used in interpretation algorithms. Interpretation, a technical concept that approximates an idea by representing a logical structure within another logical structure. Interpreter (interpreter), a programme that executes instructions written in a high-level programming language. Interpretation function, a function that assigns functions and relations to the symbols of interpreted text. Interpreted language, a programming language that performs the compilation of a programme. Often the recoding is done using a special matrix. There is a type of interpretation that involves encoding and decoding and encryption and decryption.

Interpretation related to encoding and decoding can be considered as form interpretation or formal transformation of text. There is an interpretation related to the transformation of content, called semantic interpretation. Semantic interpretation algorithms are more complex.

Semantic algorithmic word interpretation belongs to the field of artificial intelligence, to machine translation [376]. In a narrow sense of the word, this technology can be considered as information interaction. In an intermediate sense, this procedure is related to cognitive technologies and cognitive information processing [377]. In addition, there is a statistical text processing [378] and cognitive information retrieval strand, which are also related to issues of semantic interpretation. Computational linguistics [379] also deals with issues of semantic interpretation In general, it should be stated that there are many approaches to information and semantic interpretation on the one hand. However, most of the close works such as "semantic interpretation in computer-aided text analysis systems" [380] are related to text and natural language. [380] refer to text and natural language. On the other hand there is no unity or even generalisation of these issues from the position of a unified theory. The issue of interpretation of artificial languages and information languages remains insufficiently investigated

A large class of spatial information processing algorithms is related to the solution of forward and backward serif [381] or, in general, forward and backward problems [382, 383]. The forward serif determines the coordinates of objects on the terrain. Reverse serif determines the characteristics of the survey point. In the second case, the reference points are used, the coordinates of which are known on the image and on the terrain.

Spatial problems are often encountered in real life. Spatial problems occur in land use, in engineering, in space exploration, and in terrestrial navigation. Spatial problems exist in military science, crystallography, beam diagnostics, and artificial intelligence. Spatial problems are solved in geodesy photogrammetry, geoinformatics and Earth remote sensing. Spatial problems are solved in psychology and cognitive science. The connecting science of spatial problem solving is geometry. It is on geometric principles that algorithms for solving spatial problems are built. Spatial problems arise in the study of the problem of comet and asteroid hazards [384]. Obtaining spatial knowledge is often associated with solving spatial problems. Spatial problem solving facilitates the transformation of implicit knowledge into explicit knowledge. Spatial problems are solved when creating virtual and augmented reality. spatial problems are solved in professional education when teaching many disciplines. Nowadays spatial problems are solved using logical methods, which led to the emergence and development of spatial logic. At present, spatial problems are solved using spatial logic, especially since logic serves as the basis for the construction of algorithms.

Spatial information is characterised by the presence of an information situation as a certain set of related objects. Accordingly, algorithms of situational information processing [385] and situational computing [386] are used.

The information situation exists in the field of computing. In the field of

The information situation is grouped in three qualitative forms. It can be considered as a condition for solving a computational problem. It can be considered as a strategy for solving a computational problem. It can be considered as an operational environment of the computational process and serve as a tool to control the computational process

A model of computation is a rather broad concept and it is interpreted as a related set of admissible operations used for computation and as a model of transaction costs of computation. It is synonymous with the term computational model. A computational situation is interpreted as a set of admissible algorithmic information situations used for computation.

The information situation is beginning to be applied in information processing and in the construction of algorithms. It describes an object that is in certain relations and connections with the environment. The information situation can be interpreted as a microenvironment if it is changeable. The information situation as a microenvironment always acts as an addition to the main object of research. The information situation can be constructed in the real space and in the parameter space. When solving problems and organising calculations, the information situation can have qualitatively different meanings. For example, an information situation is a condition for solving a problem. Information situation as a result of solution. Information situation as a solution process. Information situation as a state. In [387] they introduce a new notion "information computational situation". Why informational computational and not computational situation? A computational situation can describe the process of computation without regard to conditions. A computational situation can describe the state of a technical means, such as stopping, freezing, looping, and others. A computational situation may describe the state of a computation process. An information computing situation informs about the conditions of information processing and makes it possible to associate the results of information processing (including calculations) with the processing conditions.

Another direction of algorithms is related to the processing of photogrammetric information [388]. In this case, photogrammetric processing based on the principles of geometric logic and image processing [389-391] based on the principles of pattern recognition are divided.

Spatial information processing algorithms are not a homogeneous direction, but are divided into several directions.

1.  A scientific direction based on the integration of geometry, computer science and Earth sciences, studying spatial and temporal phenomena in real space.

2.  Applied direction aimed at developing practical solutions related to the development of society (resource allocation, territory and transport management).

3.  Production of special-purpose technical means (information-measuring systems, geodetic tools, computer programmes). The central element of spatial problem solving is spatial relations

4.  Artificial intelligence area related to spatial knowledge

5.  the field of psychology concerned with spatial thinking.

6.  The field of cognitive science related to cognitive pattern recognition

7.  The field of spatial logic. Related to construction and design.

8.  Area of monitoring of spatial objects

9.  Area of rocket engineering, Related to trajectory calculations

10. The field of robotics related to stereo vision of robots

11. The field of transport related to unmanned driving

Representing solutions to spatial problems often uses digital and cartographic representations.

Thus, the development and modernisation of spatial information processing algorithms is an actual scientific direction and requires further research.

Literature

1. Tikhonov A.N., Ivannikov A.D., Tsvetkov V.Y. Terminological relations // Fundamental Research. -2009. - № 5. - c.146- 148

2. Gospodinov S.G. Information Fields in Space Research // Russian Journal of Astrophysical Research. Series A, 2023,9(1). C. 10-13

3. Tsvetkov V. Ya. Natural and artificial information field// International Journal of Applied and Fundamental Research. -2014. - №5-2. - c.178 -180

4. Tsvetkov V.Ya. Information field and information space // International Journal of Applied and Fundamental Research. - 2016. - №1-3. - c.455-456.

5. Chekharin E.E., Tsvetkov V.Ya. Cognitive semantics in the information field // Slavic Forum, 2015. - 4(10) - c.348-356.

6. Savinykh V.P. Opposition analysis in the information field // Slavic Forum, 2016. -3(13). - c.236-241.

7. Tsvetkov V. Ya. Information Space, Information Field, Information Environment // European researcher. 2014. № 8-1(80). p.1416-1422/

8. Dzhorova S. M. Attribute analysis of the information field geoinformatics // Slavic Forum. 2023, 2(40). C. 67-80.

9. Tsvetkov V.Ya. Discrete modelling in the information field // Slavic Forum. 2023, 1(39). C.177-182.

10. Buchkin V.A. Spatial aspects of the information field // Slavic Forum. 2023, 2(40). C. 257-268

11. Elsukov P.Y. Extraction of hidden knowledge in information technology field // Slavic Forum. - 2017. -3(17). - c.54-61.

12. Kudzh S.A. Information Field: Monograph. - MOSCOW: MAKS Press, 2017. - 97 c.

13. Tsvetkov V.Ya. Terminological field // International journal of applied and fundamental research. - 2016. - №3-3. - c.503.

14. Tsvetkov V.Ya. Formation of definitions // International Journal of Applied and Fundamental Research. - 2016. - №3-3. - c.503-504

15. Tikhonov A.N., Tsvetkov V.Ya. Methods and Systems of Decision Support. - Moscow: MAKS Press, 2001. -312c

16. Tsvetkov V.Ya. Logic in science and methods of evidence - Moscow: MGOU, 2012.- 68 p.

17. Tsvetkov V.Ya. Logic in science and methods of evidence. - LAP LAMBERT Academic Publishing GmbH & Co. KG, Saarbrucken, 2012. -84 c.

18. Kudzh C.A., Tsvetkov V.Y. Laws of the information field. - Moscow: MAKS Press, 2017. - 80 c

19. Floridi L. What is the Philosophy of Information? //Metaphilosophy. - 2002. - T. 33. - №. 1-2. - C. 123-145.

20. Floridi L. The philosophy of information. - OUP Oxford, 2013.

21. Floridi L. The logic of information: A theory of philosophy as conceptual design. - Oxford University Press, 2019.

22. Ivannikov A.D., Tikhonov A.H., Soloviev I.V., Tsvetkov V.Ya. Infosphere and Infology. - M: TORUS PRESS, 2013. -176 c.

23. Tsvetkov V.Ya. Hypothesis about the evolution of the term "information" // Perspectives of science and education - 2014. - №6 (12). - c.9-13

24. Meyns C. (ed.). Information and the History of Philosophy. - Routledge, 2021.

25. Khasanov E. Explicit and implicit derivation // JSPI Archive of Scientific Publications. - 2020.

26. Buyanova L. Yu. Terminological derivation in the language of science: cognitiveness, semioticity, functionality. - Limited Liability Company FLINTA, 2011. - C. 389-389.

27. Todosienko 3. V. Semantic derivation as the most important
mechanism of the content dynamics of language (on the material of Russian and English languages) // Fundamental Studies. - 2014. - T. 3. - №. 5.

28. Vanyagina M. R. Algorithmisation of teaching foreign language grammar at a higher military school // Letters to Emission. Offline. - 2022. - №. 6. - C. 3083.

29. Sokolova E. S., Razinkin K. A. Algorithmisation of multi-agent
reinforcement learning in game-theoretic optimal strategy search problems // Modelling, Optimization and Information Technologies. - 2020. - T. 8. - №. 1. - C. 21-22.

30. Poryvaeva N. F. Algorithmisation of Law and Principles of Law
//Society: politics, economics, law. - 2021. - №. 4 (93). - C. 67-69.

31. Kuj S.A., Tsvetkov V.Y. Logic and algorithms. - Moscow: MAKS Press, 2019. - 112 c.

32. Serikh L. V., Kondakov V. L., Voloshina L. N. Algorithm
Design and implementation of technology of preschoolers' socialisation in motor-play activity // Modern Problems of Science and Education. - 2020. - №. 5. - C. 18-18.

33. Schennikov A. N. Logical situations in the design of algorithms // Slavic Forum. - 2018. - №. 3. - C. 137-143.

34. Filippova A. S., Valiakhmetova Y. I., Dyaminova E. I.
Design of geometric placement algorithms based on matrix and level technologies // Vestnik of Ufa State Aviation Technical University. - 2016. - T. 20. - №. 4 (74). - C. 114124.

35. Tsvetkov V.Ya. Problem solving using systemic
analysis // Perspectives of Science and Education - 2015. - №1(13). - c.50-55.

36. Kudzh S.A., Tsvetkov V.Y. System approach in dissertation research // Prospects of Science and Education-2014. - №3(9). - c.26-32.

37. Tsvetkov V.Y. Theory of systems. - Moscow: MAKS Press, 2018. - 88 c.

38. Mesarovich M., Takahara N. General theory of systems: mathematical foundations. - M.: Mir, 1978 -311 pp.

39. Kuj S. A. Systemic approach // Slavic Forum. - 2014. - 1(5). - c.252 -257.

40. Kozlov, A.V. Systemic analysis of subsidiary systems // Slavic Forum. -2019. - 1(23). - c.116-122.

41. Matchin, V.T. System analysis at updating the database // Slavic Forum. - 2019. - 1(23). - c.123-130.

42. Oznamets V.V. System analysis of geodetic support // ITNOU: Information technologies in science, education and management. - 2019. - № 1(11). - c. 53-55.

43. Kolmogorov A., Fomin S. Elements of the theory of functions and A functional analysis. - Litres, 2018/.

44. Yosida K. Functional analysis. - Springer Science & Business Media, 2012.

45. Conway J. B. A course in functional analysis. - Springer, 2019. - T. 96.

46. Dieudonne J. History of Functional Analyais //Functional Analysis, Holomorphy, and Approximation Theory. - CRC Press, 2020. - C. 119-129.

47. Yurkovetskiy L. et al. Structural and functional analysis of the D614G SARS-CoV-2 spike protein variant //Cell. - 2020. - T. 183. - №. 3. - C. 739-751. e8.

48. Nomokonova O. Yu. Types of information correspondences // Slavic Forum. -2018. - 2(20). - c.44-49.

49. Tsvetkov V.Ya. Information compliance // International Journal of applied and fundamental research. - 2016. - №1 - 3. - c.454-455.

50. Tsvetkov V.Ya. Relation, connection, correspondence // Slavic Forum, 2016. -2(12). - c.272-276.

51. Tsvetkov V.Ya., Chekharin E.E. Information conformity at the information interactions // Slavic Forum. - 2017. -3(17). - c.8388.

52. Ozherel'eva T.A. Information compliance and information morphism in the information field // ITNOU: Information Technologies in Science, Education and Management. - 2017. -№4. - c.86-92

53. Bulgakov, S.V. Information correspondence in geoinformation modelling // Slavic Forum. - 2017. -4(18). - p.7- 13yu

54. Voishvillo E.K. Principle of correspondence as a form of knowledge development and the concept of relative truth. Critique of the concept of incommensurability

of successive theories. // Logic and V.E.K.: Collection of scientific works: To
the 90th anniversary of the birth of Prof. Voyshvillo Evgeny Kazimirovin. - M.:
Sovremennye tetradi, 2003. - c.11 -21.
55. Tyagunov A.M., Tsvetkov V.Ya. Logic of space observations //
Russian Journal of Astrophysical Research. Series A, 2021,7(1): 43-48
56. Bolbakov R.G. Descriptive logic in the information field //
Slavic Forum. -2018. - 3(21). - c.62-67.
57. Bolbakov, R.G.; Tsvetkov, V.Ya. Abductive inference // Slavic
Forum. -2018. - 3(21). - c.68-72.
58. Nomokonova O.Yu. Uncertainty and ternary logic //
Slavic Forum. -2018. - 3(21). - c.108-113.
59. Oznamets V.V. Logic of geodetic support // Slavic Forum. -2018. - 3(21). -
c.114-119.
60. Nomokonova O.Yu. Probabilistic logic in diagnostics //
Slavic Forum. -2019. - 2(24). - c.44-50
61. Elsukov P. Yu. Cognitive logic // Slavic Forum. -2020. -
3(29). -c.87-95.
62. Nomokonov I. B. Spatial logic in radial diagnostics // Slavic Forum. -2020. -
3(29). -c.129-139.
63. Tyagunov A.M., Tsvetkov V.Ya. Probabilistic Logic in the
Algorithmisation // Slavic Forum. 2021, 2(32). C.234-243.
64. Tsvetkov, V.Ya. Algorithmic logic // Slavic Forum. 2021,
4(34). C. 142-150
65. Tsvetkov V.Ya. Argumentation and logic // Slavic Forum. 2022,
2(36). C. 163-174
66. Tsvetkov V.Ya. Cognitive logic // ITNOU: Information technologies in
science, education and management. - 2019. - № 1(11). - c. 106-110.
67. Tsvetkov V.Ya. Spatial knowledge and spatial logic // ITNOU: Information
technologies in science, education and management. - 2019. - № 3 (13). - c.17-
26.
68. Rogov I.E. Logic and algorithms of information processing - LAP Lambert
Academic Publishing, 2019. -113 c. ISBN 978-620-0-46317-3
69. Tsvetkov V.Ya. Spatial logic in geoinformatics // Vector GeoSciences. 2020.
T. 3. № 2. C. 91-100.
70. Tsvetkov V. Ya. Application of temporal logic to update information
constructs // Slavic Forum. -2015. - 1(7) - c.286-292.
71. Kozlov A.V., Tsvetkov V.Ya. Decision-making support with
application of intuitionistic logic // Slavic Forum. -2018. - 3(21). - c.93-98.
72. Tsvetkov V.Ya. Elements of cognitive logic // Slavic Forum.

2021, 2(32). C.244-250

73. Savinykh V.P. Development of cognitive logic// Slavic Forum.
2021, 3(33). C. 140-155.

74. Buravtsev A.V. Use of interval temporal Allen logic in complex organisational and technical systems // Informatisation of education and science. - 2018, -№ 1(37). - C. 93-103.

75. Ozherelieva T. A. Application of probabilistic logic in the testing // ITNOU: Information Technologies in Science, Education and Management. - 2019. - № 1(11). - c. 8-16

76. Tyagunov A. M. Algorithms of probabilistic and spatial of logic. - Saarbruken, 2021. -153 c. ISBN 978-620-3-91161-9

77. Tsvetkov V.Ya. Logics of algorithm construction. - Saarbruken, 2021. - 109 c.

78. Tsvetkov V.Y., Ismas D.M. Development of cognitive logic // Proceedings of IX International Scientific Conference "IT - STANDARD 2019. - c.171-175

79. Kozlov, A.V.; Titov, E.K. Areas of applicability of non sequential algorithms (in Russian) // IT - Standard. 2021. 4(29). c.45-50

80. S.G. Gospodinov Logical Reasoning in Scientific Research // ITNOU: Information Technologies in Science, Education and Management. - 2018. - № 6 (10). -C. 41-48.

81. Mirkowska G., Salwicki A. Algorithmic logic. - Springer Science & Business Media, 1987.

82. Onwuegbuzie A. J. J., Leech N. L., Collins K. M. T. Qualitative analysis techniques for the review of the literature //Qualitative Report. - 2012. - T. 17. - C. 56.

83. Ezzy D. Qualitative analysis. - Routledge, 2013.

84. Raev V. K. Qualitative analysis using preference theory// Slavic Forum. - 2019. - 2(24). - c. 57-64

85. Matchin V.T., Tsvetkov V.Ya. Qualitative analysis // Slavic Forum. -2020. - 3(29). -c.205-213.

86. Rose R., Mackenzie W. J. M. Comparing forms of comparative analysis //Political studies. - 1991. - T. 39. - №. 3. - C. 446-462.

87. Kuj C.A. Oppositional comparative analysis // Slavic Forum. -2020. - 1(27). -c.38-47

88. Nomokonova O. Yu. Dichotomous comparative analysis in the medical diagnostics // Slavic Forum. -2020. - 1(27). -c.59-66

89. Aliboeva N. The expression of comparative analysis //Science and innovation. - 2022. - T. 1. - №. B7. - C. 93-95.

90. Ivannikov A.D., Tikhonov A.H., Mordvinov V.A. Knowledge acquisition

by methods of informatics and geoinformatics // Bulletin of Moscow State Regional University. - 2012. - №3. - c 140-142.

91. Tsvetkov V.Ya. Knowledge extraction for the formation of information resources. - M.: GNII IOT. 2006. - 158 c.

92. Bolbakov R. G., Tsvetkov V.Ya. G., Tsvetkov V.Y. Knowledge extraction in the information field // Slavic Forum. 2021, 4(34). C. 171-179

93. Tsvetkov V.Ya. Obtaining knowledge in the information field. - Saarbruken, 2021. -193 c.

94. Solov'ev I.V., Tsvetkov V.Ya. On the content and interrelations of categories "information", "information resources", "knowledge" // Distance and Virtual Learning. - 2011. - №6 (48) - c.11-21

95. Gospodinov S.G. Modern Informatics. - Saarbruken, 2023. - 157 c.

96. Polyakov A.A., Tsvetkov V.Ya. Applied Informatics. - M.: Janus-K, 2002. - 392 c.

97. Kozlov A.V., Rogov A.V. Algorithm as a tool of extraction knowledge // Slavic Forum. 2021, 4(34). C.30-41.

98. Ozherel'eva T.A. Logical techniques and methods used in knowledge extraction // ITNOU: Information Technologies in Science, Education and Management. - 2018. - № 6 (10). -C.69-77

99. Kuzhelev P. D. Spatial knowledge for transport management // State Counsellor. - 2016. - №2. - c 17-22.

100.	Tsvetkov V.Ya. Formation of spatial knowledge: Monograph. - Moscow: MAKS Press, 2015. - 68 c.

101.	Ivannikov, A.D. Knowledge extraction by methods of geoinformatics// Slavic Forum. -2020. - 4(30). -c.262-272.

102.	Tsvetkov V.Ya. Implicit knowledge and its varieties // Vestnik Mordovian University. - 2014. - T. 24. № 3. - c.199-205

103.	Tsvetkov V. Ya. Analysis of implicit knowledge // Perspectives of science and Education. - 2014. - №1 (7). - c.56-60

104.	Kuj S. A. Implicit knowledge in the information field // Slavic Forum. -2018. - 3(21). - c.14-20

105.	Elsukov P.Y. Extraction of implicit knowledge in educational programmes technologies // Slavic Forum. 2021, 1(31). C.112-125

106.	Savinykh V.P. Explicit and implicit knowledge // Slavic Forum. -2020. - 2(28). -c.103-111.

107.	Tsvetkov V. Ya. The language of informatics // Uspekhi sovremennoi

Natural Science. - 2014. - №7. - c.129-133.

108.   Raev V.K. Information units in the information sciences //
Educational Resources and Technology. - 2022. - № 1 (38). - C. 68-75.

109.   Tsvetkov V. Ya. Semantics of information units // Uspekhi
of modern natural science. - 2007. - №10. - c.103-104.

110.   Todorova A.I. Theory of information units // In Collection:
Modern information technologies. Collection of scientific articles of the 9th
International Scientific and Technical Conference. Burgas, 2023. C. 220-228.

111.   Frans H. Van Eemeran, Rob Grootendorst (2004). "A Systematic Theory
of Argumentation". Published by the Press Syndicate of the University of
Cambridge. Philosophy: 12.

112.   Ihnen Jory C. Negotiation and deliberation: Grasping the difference
//Argumentation. - 2016. - T. 30. - №. 2. - C. 145-165.

113.   33. Tsvetkov V. Ya. Information interaction // European researcher.
2013. № 11-1 (62). C. 2573-2577

114.   Tsvetkov V.Ya. Information impact and interaction //
Slavic Forum. -2020. - 4(30). -c.144-151

115.   Van Eemeren F. H. et al. Handbook of argumentation theory. A
comprehensive overview of the state of the art. - 2014.

116.   Tsvetkov V.Ya. Logic in science and methods of evidence. - Saarbrucken,
2012. -84 c.

117.   Gordon T. F., Prakken H., Walton D.. The Carneades model of argument
and burden of proof //Artificial Intelligence. - 2007. - T. 171. - №. 10-15. - C.
875896

118.   Raev V.K., Tsvetkov V.Ya. Logical chains // Distance and
Virtual learning. 2018. - № 1(120). - c.14-21

119.   Walton, Douglas; Krabbe, E. C. W. (1995). Commitment in Dialogue:
Basic Concepts of Interpersonal Reasoning. Albany: SUNY Press

120.   Psathas, George (1995): Conversation Analysis, Thousand Oaks: Sage
Sacks, Harvey. (1995). Lectures on Conversation. Blackwell Publishing

121.   Gross A. G. The rhetoric of science. - Harvard University Press, 1990.

122.   Jacques Ellul, Propaganda, Vintage, 1973.

123.   Tsvetkov V.Ya. Information field and information field
space // International Journal of Applied and Fundamental Research. - 2016. -
№1-3. - c.455-456.

124.   Toulmin, Stephen E. (1958). The Uses of Argument. Cambridge
University Press. ISBN 978-0521092302.

125.   Charles Arthur Willard. "Some Questions About Toulmin's View of
Argument Fields." Jack Rhodes and Sara Newell, eds. Proceedings of the

Summer Conference on Argumentation. 1980. "Field Theory: A Cartesian Meditation." George Ziegelmueller and Jack Rhodes, eds. Dimensions of Argument: Proceedings of the Second Summer Conference on Argumentation.

126. G. T. Goodnight, "The Personal, Technical, and Public Spheres of Argument." Journal of the American Forensics Association. (1982) 18:214-227.

127. Bruce E. Gronbeck. "Sociocultural Notions of Argument Fields: A Primer." George Ziegelmueller and Jack Rhodes, eds. Dimensions of Argument: Proceedings of the Second Summer Conference on Argumentation. (1981) 1-20.

128. Van Eemeren F. H. et al. Handbook of argumentation theory. A comprehensive overview of the state of the art. - 2014.

129. See Ray E. McKerrow. "Argument Communities: A Quest for Distinctions

130. Walton, Douglas (2013). Methods of Argumentation. Cambridge: Cambridge University Press.

131. Walton, Douglas; Reed, Chris; Macagno, Fabrizio (2008). Argumentation Schemes. New York: Cambridge University Press

132. David Zarefsky. "Product, Process, or Point of View? Jack Rhodes and Sara Newell, ed.s Proceedings of the Summer Conference on Argumentation. 1980.

133. Walton D., Zhang N. The epistemology of scientific evidence //Artificial Intelligence and Law. - 2013. - T. 21. - №. 2. - C. 173-219.

134. Tsvetkov V. Ya. Information Constructions // European Journal of Technology and Design. -2014. № 3(5). - p.147-152

135. Anderson R. L., Mortensen C. D. Logic and marketplace argumentation //Quarterly Journal of Speech. - 1967. - T. 53. - №. 2. - C. 143-151.

136. Tsvetkov V. Ya. Information Constructions // European Journal of Technology and Design. -2014. № 3(5). - p.147-152.

137. Tsvetkov, V.Ya. The use of oppositional variables to analyse the quality of educational services (in Russian) // Sovremennye naukoyemkie tekhnologii. - 2008. - №1. - c.62-64.

138. Savinykh V.P. Opposition analysis in the information field // Slavic Forum, 2016. -3(13). - c.236-241.

139. Tsvetkov V.Ya. Dichotomous analysis of system complexity // Perspectives of Science and Education - 2014. - №2 (8). - c.15-20.

140. Kuj, S.A. Dichotomous structural analysis // Slavic Forum. - 2017. -2(16). - c.7-11.

141. Domashuk P.V. Algorithm for assessing the corruption component in bidding // Slavic Forum, 2015. - 2(8) - c.68 - 74.

142. Tsvetkov V.Y., Nomokonova O.Yu. Algorithmic diagnostics of cough //

Medicine and High Technologies. 2017. - 2. - c.5357.

143. Bogoutdinov B.B., Tsvetkov V.Ya. Application of complementary resources model in investment activity // Vestnik of Mordovian University. - 2014. - T. 24. № 4. - c.103-116.

144. Averina T. A. Statistical algorithm for modelling dynamic systems with variable structure // Siberian Journal of Computational Mathematics. - 2002. - T. 5. - №. 1. - C. 1-10

145. Selmanova N.N., Tsvetkov V.Y. Application of statistical method for calculating the area of areal object // Perspectives of Science and Education. - 2018. - №1(31). - c.55-60.

146. Galaev A. B. et al. Logico-statistical algorithm for identification through pores and its application for analysing nanomaterial structure // Applied Informatics. - 2013. - №. 2 (44). - c42-48.

147. Cormen T. et al. Algorithms. Construction and analysis. - Publisher's Williams House, 2009.

148. Tsvetkov V.Ya. Algorithms for solving direct and inverse spatial task. // Informatisation and Communication. - 2017. - №2. - c.71-75.

149. Cormen, Thomas H.; Leiserson, Charles E.; Rivest, Ronald L. Introduction to Algorithms.- 1st.- MIT Press and McGraw-Hill, 1990.- 863p. ISBN 0-262-03141-8.

150. Nechepurenko M. I. I., Popkov V. K., Mainagashev S. M. Algorithms and Programmes for solving problems on graphs and networks. - Nauka, Sib. department, 1990.

151. Mathematics. Large Encyclopaedic Dictionary /Editor-in-Chief Yu. Prokhorov. 3rd ed. - Moscow: Big Russian Encyclopaedia, 2000. - 848c.

152. https://ru.wikipedia.org/wiki/anropHTM data view 14.06.2023.

153. https://gtmarket.ru/concepts/7178/ data view 14.06.2023.

154. Tsvetkov V.Ya., Cheharin E.E. Algorithm of linear semantic interpretation // Slavic Forum. - 2017. -1(15). - c.134-140.

155. Chekharin E. E. Algorithms for interpretation of remote sensing data // Slavic Forum. - 2015. - №. 3. - C. 301-308..

156. Tsvetkov V.Ya., Cheharin E.E. Algorithm of informational interpretation // Informatisation and communication. - 2017. - №2. - c.76-80.

157. Bolbakov R.G. Development and application of cognitive-semantic methods and algorithms in multimedia educational portal systems. D.D.Sc. speciality 05.13.01. - M.:MIREA, 2013. - 136c.

158. I. P. Deshko, K.G. Kryazhenkov, E.E. Cheharin. Virtual Technologies // Modeling of Artificial Intelligence. 2016, Vol. 9, Is. 1, pp. 33-43. DOI: 10.13187/mai.2016.9.33 www.ejournal11.com

159. Tsvetkov V. Ya. Virtual Modeling // European Journal of Technology and Design, 2016, 1(11), pp. 35-44.

160. Tanenbaum E., M. van Steen. .Distributed Systems. Principles and paradigms - SPb.: Peter, 2003. - 877c.

161. Karpov Yu. G. Model checking. Verification of parallel and distributed software systems. - BHV-Peterburg, 2010.

162. Tsvetkov V. Ya. Cognitive Science of Information Retrieval // European Journal of Psychological Studies, 2015, 1(5). - p.37-44

163. Rosenberg I.N. Complexity of information retrieval //
Educational resources and technology. - 2017. - №1 (18). - c.41-49/

164. Moiseev N. Algorithms of development. - Moscow: Nauka, 1987. - 304c. Republished 2017, by Litres Publishers

165. Tsvetkov V. Ya. Algorithms as a means of cognition // Information Technologies. - 2018. - 8 ( 24). - c.507-515.

166. Kiryushkin M. V. Algorithmically oriented jurisprudence //.
Ros.jurid. juri. - 2007. - №. 3. - C. 19.

167. Istomin V. V. Algorithm of behaviour of groups of autonomous Intelligent agents for biomedical systems based on the theory of swarm intelligence //Pricaspian Journal: Management and High Technologies. - 2013. - №. 3. - C. 054-063.

168. Tsvetkov V.Ya. Corporate governance: monograph. - Sofia. 2023. - 123 c.

169. Tsvetkov V. Ya. Corporate governance // Modern Management Technologies. 2022. 4(100)

170. Bronnikov S.V. Corporate group management of spacecraft flight // Slavic Forum. 2022, 2(36). C. 60-67.

171. Shtovba S. D. Ant algorithms //ExponentaPro. Maths in Applications. - 2003. - T. 4. - C. 70-75.

172. Tsvetkov V.Ya., Kozlov A.V. Using models of living organisms to analyse the evolution of complex organisational and technical systems // Educational Resources and Technologies. - 2019. - №4 (29). - c.68-76

173. Tsvetkov V.Ya. Structural analysis based on living systems algorithms // Biogeosystem Technique. 2016. № 1 (7). C. 87-95.

174. Tsvetkov V.Ya. Incremental solution of the second kind problem on the example of living system // Biosciences Biotechnology Research Asia. 2014. T. 11. № S. C. 177-180.

175. Zvenigorodskaya L. A., Samsonova H. G., Toporkov A. C.
Chronic ischaemic disease of the digestive organs: algorithm of diagnostics and treatment //RMZh. - 2010. - T. 18. - №. 9. - C. 544-548.

176. Karavaeva E. V. Recommended algorithm for designing higher education programmes // Higher Education in Russia. V. Recommended algorithm for designing higher education programmes // Higher Education in Russia. - 2014. - №. 89. - c.5-15.

177. Rogov I. E. Development of algorithms for training systems // Slavic Forum. -2019. - 3(25). - c.56-66.

178. Tsvetkov V.Ya., Obolyayeva N.M. Using correlative approach for personnel management of educational institution // Distance and virtual learning. - 2011. - №8. - c.4- 9.

179. Rogov, I.E. Processing of cognitive information // Slavic Forum. -2020. - 4(30). -c.378-385

180. Rogov I.E. Methods and algorithms of educational processing information // Slavic Forum. 2021, 1(31). C.211-227.

181. Kulagin V. P., Tsvetkov V.Ya Features of multilevel testing // Distance and Virtual Learning. - 2013. - №4. -c.5-12.

182. Rogov I.E. Analysis of testing models and systems // Educational resources and technology. - 2019. - №4 (29). - c.53-60

183. Kulagin V.P., Tsvetkov V.Y. Models of multilevel testing // Informatisation of education and science. - 2013.- № 3. - c 95-101.

184. Matchin V.T., Rogov I.E. Life cycle of software Support of learning systems // Educational Resources and Technologies. - 2020. - № 1 (30). - C. 49-57.

185. Rogov I.E. Algorithmic analysis of the testing technologies - LAP Lambert Academic Publishing, 2019. -121 c.

186. Lord, F.M. (1980). Applications of item response theory to practical testing problems. Mahwah, NJ: Lawrence Erlbaum Associates, Inc.

187. Tsvetkov V.Ya. Application of response theory// Slavic Forum. - 2018. - 1(19). - c.77-81.

188. Tsvetkov, V.Ya.; Voinova, E.V. Modification of the Rasch model for estimation of free testing // Bulletin of Ryazan State Radio Engineering University. - 2018.- №1(63). - c.90-94.

189. Thissen, D. & Orlando, M. (2001). Item response theory for items scored in two categories. In D. Thissen & Wainer, H. (Eds.), *Test Scoring* (pp. 73-140). Mahwah, NJ: Lawrence Erlbaum Associates, Inc.

190. de Ayala, R.J. (2009). The Theory and Practice of Item Response Theory, New York, NY: The Guilford Press. (6.12), p.144.

191. Tsvetkov V.Ya. Directions of testing in the sphere of education // Modern additional professional pedagogical education. - 2017. - № 2. - c.72 -80.

192. Nomokonova O. Yu. Structural modelling of social factors // Slavic

Forum. - 2017. -2(16). - c.57-61.

193.   Lytneva N. A., Komarevtseva O.. O. Algorithm of financial and investment assessment of municipal education for the study of economic systems efficiency // International Journal of Applied and Fundamental Research. - 2015. - №. 11-2. - C. 290-295.

194.   Samarsky A. A. Mathematical modelling and computational experiment //Vestnik An USSR. - 1979. - T. 5. - c.469-486.

195.   Tsvetkov V. Ya. Algorithm of qualitative information processing in preference assessment // Slavic Forum, 2016. -4(14). - c.268-274.

196.   Buravtsev, A.V. Complex technological systems// Slavic Forum. - 2017. -4(18). - c.14-19.

197.   Ozherel'eva T.A. Descriptive models // International Journal of Applied and Fundamental Research. - 2016. - №5. (Part 4) - p. 675- 675

198.   Tsvetkov V.Ya. Descriptive and prescriptive information models // Distance and Virtual Learning-2015. - №7. - c.48- 54.

199.   TsvetkovV. Ya. Information Asymmetry as a Risk Factor // European researcher. Series A. 2014, Vol.(86), No. 11-1, pp. 1937-1943.

200.   Tsvetkov V. Ya. Evaluations of Information Asymmetry // Modern Applied Science; 2015; № 6 (9); pp.243-247.

201.   Tsvetkov V.Ya. Information asymmetry in education // Distance and virtual learning-2015. - №5. - c.4- 12.

202.   Obolyayeva N.M. Elimination of information asymmetry as a tool to improve the quality of education // Izvestiya vysshee obrazovaniya vysshee obrazovaniya. Geodesy and aerial photography. - 2012. - №6. - c. 123 - 124.

203.   Matchin V. A. Uncertainty as a factor of necessity updating databases // Educational Resources and Technologies - 2017. -2 (19). - c.98-104.

204.   Nomokonova O. Yu. Information uncertainty in information interaction // Slavic Forum. - 2017. -1(15). - c. 104110.

205.   Tsvetkov V.Ya. Information uncertainty and certainty in information sciences // Information Technologies. - 2015. - №1. -c.3-7

206.   Rogov, I.E.; Tsvetkov, V.Ya. Algorithms of the first and second kind // Slavic Forum. -2020. - 4(30). -c.105-116.

207.   Tsvetkov V.Ya. Complexity of algorithms of the first kind // Educational Resources and Technologies. - 2020. - № 4 (33). - C. 73-80.

208.   Schennikov, A.E. Models of direct algorithms // Slavic Forum. - 2017. -4(18). - c.103-109.

209. Tsvetkov V.Ya., Kozlov A.. V. Algorithm of subsidiary metaheuristics // Educational Resources and Technologies. - 2022. - № 4 (41). - C.87-95.

210. Tsvetkov, V.Ya. Solving problems of the second kind using an information approach // International Journal of Applied and fundamental research. - 2014. - №11-2. - c.191-195

211. Nonaka, I. (1994). A dynamic theory of organisational knowledge creation. *Organisation Science*, 5(1), 14-37/

212. Tsvetkov, V.Ya. Implicit knowledge in space research. Perspectives of science and education - 2015. - №4(16). - c.19-27

213. Tsvetkov V.Ya. Implicit knowledge in education // International Journal of applied and fundamental research. - 2016. - №3-3. - c.504505.

214. Sigov A.S., Tsvetkov V.Y. Implicit knowledge: oppositional logical analysis and typologisation // Bulletin of the Russian Academy of Sciences, 2015, Vol. 85, No. 9, - p.800-804.

215. Tsvetkov V. Ya. Information Situation and Information Position as a Management Tool // European researcher. 2012, 12-1 (36), p.2166- 2170.

216. Potapov A. S. Information situation and information situation position in the information field // Slavic Forum. - 2017. - 1(15). - c.283289.

217. Rosenberg I.N., Tsvetkov V.Y. Information situation. // International Journal of Applied and Basic Research. - 2010. - 12. - c.126-127.

218. Ozherelieva T.A. Information situation as a management tool // Slavic Forum, 2016. -4(14). - c. 176-181.

219. Tsvetkov V.Ya. Model of information situation // Prospects Science and Education. - 2017. - №3(27). - c.13-19.

220. Tsvetkov, V.Ya. Systematics of information situations // Perspectives on science and education. - 2016. - №5(23). - c.64-68.

221. Selmanova N.N. Information situation as a tool real estate valuation // Slavic Forum. -2018. - 2(20). - c.90-96.

222. Ozherel'eva T. A. Structural analysis of management systems // State Advisor. - 2015. - №1. - c40-44.

223. Polyakov A. A., Tsvetkov V. Ya. Information Technologies in Management. - Moscow State University, Faculty of Public Administration, 2007. - 138c.

224. Tsvetkov V.Ya. Development of management technologies // The State Counsellor. - 2015. - №4(12). - c.5-10.

225. Lototsky V.L. Principles of information management // Slavic Forum, 2016. -4(14). - c.149-154.

226. Tsvetkov V.Ya. Triad as an interpretive system. // Perspectives on science and education. - 2015. - №6. - c.18-23.

227. Kudzh S. A., Tsvetkov V. Y. Triadic comparative analysis //Journal of mechanics of continua and mathematical sciences. Special Issue. - 2020. - №. 10. - C. 745-754.

228. Jongsma, 2014 - Jongsma, C. (2014). Poythress's Trinitarian Logic: A Review Essay. // *Pro Rege, 42*(4), 6-15

229. Oleynik A. H. Triangulation in content analysis. questions methodologies and empirical verification // Sociological Research. - 2009. - №. 2. - C. 65-79.

230. Tsvetkov V.Ya. Triad as a tool of scientific analysis // Slavic Forum, 2015. - 3(9) - c.294-300.

231. Tsvetkov V.Ya. Externalisation of implicit knowledge // International Journal of applied and fundamental research. - 2016. - № 12-1. - C156-161

232. Nomokonov I.B. Externalisation of knowledge in radiation diagnostics // Slavic Forum, 2016. -2(12). - c.204-208.

233. Rosenberg, I.N.; Kozlov, A.V. Logical analysis of the control schemes (in Russian) // Slavic Forum. -2018. - 2(20). - c.83-89.

234. Tsvetkov V.Ya. Logical adherence // Slavic Forum. -2018. - 3(21). - c.126-130.

235. Schennikov A.N. Logical situations in designing algorithms // Slavic Forum. -2018. - 3(21). - c. 137-143.

236. Pavlov A.I. Logical situations and constructions // Slavic Forum. -2020. - 1(27). -c.67-76.

237. Raev V.K., Tsvetkov V.Ya. Logical chains // Distance and virtual learning. 2018. - № 1(120). - c.14-21

238. Fearnhead P., Wyncoll D., Tawn J. A sequential smoothing algorithm with linear computational cost //Biometrika. - 2010. - T. 97. - №. 2. - C. 447-464.

239. Shen Z. et al. Many sequential iterative algorithms can be parallel and (nearly) work-efficient //Proceedings of the 34th ACM Symposium on Parallelism in Algorithms and Architectures. - 2022. - C. 273-286.

240. Tsvetkov V. Ya., Matchin V. T. Information Conversion into Information Resources// European Journal of Technology and Design. - 2014. - № 2(4), p.92-104

241. Hippke M., Heller R. Optimised transit detection algorithm to search for periodic transits of small planets //Astronomy & Astrophysics. - 2019. - T. 623. - C. A39.

242. Anikina G.A., Polyakov M.G., Romanov L.N., Tsvetkov V.Ya. On the Image contour extraction using linear trained models. // Izvestia of the USSR

Academy of Sciences. Technical Cybernetics. -1980. - №6. - с.36-43

243. Lynchenko A., Sheshkus A., Arlazarov V. L. Document image recognition algorithm based on similarity metric robust to projective distortions for mobile devices //Eleventh International Conference on Machine Vision (ICMV 2018). - International Society for Optics and Photonics, 2019. - T. 11041. - C. 110411K.

244. Xingyun Q., Shaobin C., Yanwei H. An Algorithm for Identification of Inland River Shorelines based on Phase Correlation Algorithm //2019 Chinese Automation Congress (CAC). - IEEE, 2019. - C. 2047-2053.

245. Xiao Y. et al. Non-Intrusive Load Identification Method Based on Improved KM Algorithm //IEEE Access. - 2019. - T. 7. - C. 151368-151377.

246. Zhang H., Su S. A hybrid multi-agent Coordination Optimisation Algorithm //Swarm and Evolutionary Computation. - 2019. - T. 51. - C. 100603.

247. Hippke M., Heller R. Optimised transit detection algorithm to search for periodic transits of small planets //Astronomy & Astrophysics. - 2019. - T. 623. - C. A39.

248. Lynchenko A., Sheshkus A., Arlazarov V. L. Document image recognition algorithm based on similarity metric robust to projective distortions for mobile devices //Eleventh International Conference on Machine Vision (ICMV 2018). - International Society for Optics and Photonics, 2019. - T. 11041. - C. 110411K.

249. Xingyun Q., Shaobin C., Yanwei H. An Algorithm for Identification of Inland River Shorelines based on Phase Correlation Algorithm //2019 Chinese Automation Congress (CAC). - IEEE, 2019. - C. 2047-2053/

250. Xiao Y. et al. Non-Intrusive Load Identification Method Based on Improved KM Algorithm //IEEE Access. - 2019. - T. 7. - C. 151368-151377.

251. Rosenberg I.N., Tsvetkov V.Y. Application of multi-agent systems in intelligent logistic systems. // International Journal of Experimental Education. - 2012. - №6. - с.107-109.

252. Rogov I. E. Application of multi-agent systems in management transport of a megacity // Science and technology of railways. - 2020. T.4. - 1(13). - с.26-36.

253. Zhang H., Su S. A hybrid multi-agent Coordination Optimisation Algorithm //Swarm and Evolutionary Computation. - 2019. - T. 51. - C. 100603.

254. Ivannikov A. D. The problem of information languages and the current state of informatics // Vestnik MSTU MIREA. - 2014. - № 4(5). - с.39-62.

255. Herold G., Kirshanova E., May A. On the asymptotic complexity of solving LWE //Designs, Codes and Cryptography. - 2018. - T. 86. - №. 1. - C.

5583

256. Sipser M. Introduction To The Theory Of Computation, ser //Computer Science Series. Thomson Course Technology. - 2006.

257. Tsvetkov, V.Ya., Mordvinov, V.A. Approach to systematisation of algorithms // Design Ontology. - 2018. - T. 7, №4(26). - C. 388-397.

258. Raev V.K. Mythological models as a research tool // Slavic Forum. -2020. - 3(29). -c.56-66.

259. Kudzh S.A., Tsvetkov V.Y. Comparative Analysis. Moscow: MAKS Press, 2020. -144c.

260. Tsvetkov V.Ya. Proportionality as qualitative and cognitive attitude // Slavic Forum. 2021, 2(32). C.244-250.

261. Tsvetkov V.Ya. Information impact and interaction // Slavic Forum. -2020. - 4(30). -c.144-151

262. Raev V.K. Proportionality in the information field // Slavic Forum. 2021, 3(33). C. 105-114

263. Bolbakov R. G. Proportionality in geoinformatics // Slavic Forum. 2022, 4(38). C. 456-465

264. Kuj S.A., Tsvetkov V.Y. Factors of cognitive complexity // ITNOU: Information technologies in science, education and management. - 2018.- № 6 (10). -C.34-41.

265. Kuj S. A. Estimation of group cognitive complexity // Slavic Forum. - 2018. - 2(20). - c.36-43.

266. Kozlov A.V., Rogov I.E., Titov E.K., Tsvetkov V.Ya. Analiz complexity of programme components // Slavic Forum. -2020. - 4(30). - c.410-419

267. Gospodinov S.G. Theory of complex systems. - Saarbruken, 2023. -217 c.

268. Monakhov S.V., Savinykh V.P., Tsvetkov V.Ya. Methodology of Analysis and Design of Complex Information Systems. - Moscow: Prosveshchenie, 2005. - 264c.

269. Tsvetkov V. Ya. Fundamentals of the theory of complex systems: Textbook. - SPb.: Publishers "Lan", 2019. - 152 c.

270. Tsvetkov V. Ya. Information Units as the Elements of Complex Models // Nanotechnology Research and Practice. - 2014, № 1(1), p.57-64/

271. Ozhereleva T. A. Systematics for information units // European Researcher. 2014, no. 11/1 (86), pp. 1894-1900.

272. Gallo G. Conflict theory, complexity and systems approach //Systems Research and Behavioral Science. - 2013. - T. 30. - №. 2. - C. 156-175.

273. Turner J. R., Baker R. M. Complexity theory: An overview with potential

applications for the social sciences //Systems. - 2019. - T. 7. - №. 1. - C. 4.

274. Tsvetkov V.Ya. Fact-fixing and interpreting models // International Journal of Applied and Fundamental Research. - 2016. - №9-3. - c.487/

275. Savinykh V.P., Tsvetkov V.Y. Fact-fixing models //
Slavic Forum. -2019. - 3(25). - c.67-74.

276. Misra S., Akman I. Weighted class complexity: a measure of complexity for object oriented system // Journal of Information Science and Engineering. - 2008. - T. 24. - C. 1689-1708.

277. Zhao X., Feng Z. Centralised Reasoning Translation and Its Computing Complexity for Heterogeneous Semantic Mappings //International Conference on Knowledge Science, Engineering and Management. - Springer, Cham, 2019. - C. 314.

278. Papadimitriou C. H., Yannakakis M. On bounded rationality and computational complexity //Indiana University. - 1994.

279. Cobham, Alan (1965). "The intrinsic computational difficulty of functions". Proc. Logic, Methodology, and Philosophy of Science II. North Holland - 1965.

280. Schrijver A. Combinatorial optimisation: polyhedra and efficiency. - Springer Science & Business Media, 2003. - T. 24.

281. Aaronson S. A not-quite-exponential dilemma. - 2009.

282. Impagliazzo R., Paturi R. On the complexity of k-SAT // Journal of Computer and System Sciences. - 2001. - T. 62. - №. 2. - C. 367-375.

283. Tsvetkov V. Ya. Application of temporal logic to update information constructs // Slavic Forum. -2015. - 1(7) - c.286-292.

284. Teslenko P. A. Information design and attributes of its research //Problems of Technology. Scientific and Production Journal-Odessa: ONMU. - 2008. - №. 3. - C. 22-31.

285. Lototsky V.L. Information testing designs // Perspectives of science and education. - 2016. - №3. - c.32-37.

286. Melik-Gaikazyan I. V. Information processes and reality. -
M.: Nauka, 1997.

287. Pavlov A.I. Definitions as logical constructions // Slavic
Forum. -2019. - 4(26). - c.95-102.

288. Tsvetkov V.Ya., Shaitura S.V., Minitaeva A.M., Feoktistova V.M., Kozhaev Yu.P., Belyu L.P. Metamodelling in the information field // Amazonia Investiga. 2020. T. 9. № 25. C. 395-402/

289. Tsvetkov V.Y., Bulgakov S.V., Titov E.K., Rogov I.E.
Metamodelling in geoinformatics // Information and Space. 2020. - №1. -c .112-119.

290. Ozherel'eva T. A. Metamodelling and information morphism // Slavic Forum. 2021, 3(33). C.69-78.

291. Bolbakov R. G. Metamodelling in knowledge extraction //.
Slavic Forum. 2021, 4(34). C.7-17.

292. Tsvetkov, V.Ya. Dichotomous Systemic Analysis. Life Science Journal 2014; -11(6).- pp586-590.

293. Elsukov P. Yu. Paradigmatic and syntagmatic relations
In dichotomous division // Slavic Forum. - 2019. - №. 3. - C. 19-26.

294. Raev V. K. Dichotomous method of information uncertainty reduction //Perspectives of Science and Education. - 2017. - №. 2 (26).

295. Ozherel'eva T.A. Information educational constructions // Distance and virtual learning. - 2016. - №5(107). -c31-38

296. Deshko I.P. Information construction: Monograph. - M.:
MAX Press, 2016. - 64c. ISBN 978 -5-317-05244-7.

297. Mordvinov V. A., Bratus N. V., Kutuzov M. V. Semantic construction of information and methodological support of educational technologies in the instrumental environment of QR-coding // Slavic Forum. -2018. - 4 (22). - c.31-38.

298. Shaitura S.V. Modelling and construction // Slavic
Forum. -2019. - 1(23). - c.68-79.

299. Tsvetkov V.Ya. Paralinguistic information units in the
education// Perspectives of Science and Education. - 2013. - 4(4). - c.30-38.

300. Chekharin E.E. Interpretability of information units //
Slavic Forum. - 2014. - 2 (6). - c.151 -155.

301. Tsvetkov, V. Ya. Information units of messages //
Fundamental Research. - 2007. - №12-1. - c.99.

302. Rosenberg I.N., Tsvetkov V.Ya. Logical information ones
units // International Journal of Applied and Fundamental Research - 2009. - № 4. - c.110- 111.

303. Kudzh S.A., Tsvetkov V.Ya. Informational educational
units // Distance and Virtual Learning 2014. - №1(79). - c.24- 31.

304. Tsvetkov V.Ya. Information units as a means of construction
of the world picture // International Journal of Applied and Fundamental Research. - 2014. - № 8 -4. - c. 36-40.

305. Oznamets V. V. Relations of natural and artificial in the information field // Perspectives of Science and Education. - 2018. - №1(31). - c.16-22.

306. Tsvetkov, V. Ya. Worldview Model as the Result of Education // World Applied Sciences Journal. -2014. - 31 (2). - p211-215.

307. Tsvetkov V.Ya. Information description of the world picture //

Perspectives of science and education. - 2014. - №5(11). - c.9-13.

308.   Tsvetkov V.Ya. World picture as an educational paradigm //
European Social Science Journal. 2013. № 10-1 (37). - c. 28-34.

309.   Butko E.Ya. Personal picture of the world as a result of education //
Distance and virtual learning. 2017. - № 1 (115). - c.87-94.

310.   Tsvetkov V.Ya. Complementarity of information resources //
International Journal of Applied and Fundamental Research. - 2016. - №2. -
c.182-185.

311.   Tsvetkov V. Ya. Dichotomic Assessment of Information Situations and
Information Superiority // European researcher. 2014. № 11-1 (86). p.1901-
1909.

312.   Shaitura C.B. Information situation in geoinformatics//.
Educational Resources and Technology. - 2016. - №5 (17). - c. 103-108.

313.   Polyakov A.A., Tsvetkov V.Y. Applied Informatics. In 2 parts
/ Under general ed. A.N. Tikhonov - M.: MAKS Press. Vol. 1. 2008. -788 c.

314.   Kovalenko N.P. Interaction in informational
functional space // Perspectives of Science and Education. - 2016. - №2. - c.12-
16.

315.   Nilsson, N.J., 1986, Probabilistic logic// Artificial Intelligence 28(1):
7187.

316.   Josang, A., 2001, A logic for uncertain probabilities,// International
Journal of Uncertainty, Fuzziness and Knowledge-Based Systems9(3):279-311/

317.   Josang, A., 2008, " Conditional Reasoning with Subjective Logic , //
Journal of Multiple-Valued Logic and Soft Computing , 15(1), pp.5-38, 2008.

318.   Haenni, R, 2005, " Towards a Unifying Theory of Logical and
Probabilistic Reasoning // ISIPTA'05, 4th International Symposium on
Imprecise Probabilities and Their Applications: 193-202.

319.   Tsvetkov V. Ya. Logic units of information systems // Eurupean Journal
of Natural History. - 2009. - № 2. - p.99-100.

320.   Tsvetkov, V.Ya. Ergatic aspects of information processing in information
systems // Slavic Forum. - 2017. - 1(15). - c.95-103.

321.   Mordvinov V. A. Information needs of ergatic
systems// Slavic Forum. - 2017. -4(18). - c.42-49.

322.   Tsvetkov V.Ya. Ergatic aspects of information processing in GIS //
Geodesy and Aerial Photography 1999 № 3, p. 144-153

323.   Pavlov A.I. Ergatic systems // Slavic Forum. -2019. - 1(23). - c.153-159.

324.   Obolyayeva N.M. System approach to quality analysis
Education Management: Theory and Practice. - 2012. - № 3. - C.
101-105.

325. Aiello M., Pratt-Hartmann I., Van Benthem J. What is Spatial Logic? // Handbook of spatial logics. - Springer, Dordrecht, 2007. - p. 1-11

326. Rosenberg I. H., Tsvetkov V. Ya. Cognitive and spatial logic in situation centres // Science and technology of railways. - 2019. - T.3. №2(10). - c.3 -16.

327. Tsvetkov V.Ya. Spatial logic in education and science // Educational resources and technologies. - 2019. - № 2 (27). - C. 92-102

328. Tsvetkov V.Ya. Spatial knowledge and spatial logic // ITNOU: Information technologies in science, education and management. - 2019.- № 3 (13). - c. 17-26.

329. Tsvetkov V.Ya. Spatial logic in geoinformatics // Vector GeoSciences. 2020. T. 3. № 2. C. 91-100

330. Kudzh S., Tsvetkov V. Spatial logic concepts // Revista inclusions. Volumen 7. Numero Especial / Julio - Septiembre. 2020 pp. 837-849.

331. Moratz, R., & Ragni, M. Qualitative spatial reasoning about relative point position. // Journal of Visual Languages & Computing, 2008, 19(1), 75-98

332. Tsvetkov V.Ya. Qualitative spatial reasoning: Monograph. - Moscow: MAKS Press, 2017. - 60c.

333. Levin B. A., Rosenberg I. N., Tsvetkov V. Ya. Spatial logical reasoning in decision support // Railways Science and Technology. - 2018. - 4(8). - c.3 - 16/

334. Talen E. The spatial logic of parks //Journal of Urban Design. - 2010. - V.15. - №. 4. - C. 473-491.

335. Caires L., Cardelli L. A spatial logic for concurrency (part I) //Information and Computation. - 2003. - V.186. - №. 2. - C. 194-235.

336. Cardelli L., Gardner P., Ghelli G. A spatial logic for querying graphs //International Colloquium on Automata, Languages, and Programming. - Springer, Berlin, Heidelberg, 2002. - C. 597-610.

337. Del Bimbo A., Vicario E., Zingoni D. A spatial logic for symbolic description of image contents // Journal of Visual Languages & Computing. - 1994. - V.5. - №. 3. - C. 267-286.

338. Tsvetkov V. Ya. Georeference as a tool for analysing and obtaining knowledge // Earth Sciences. - 2011. - №2. - c.63-65

339. Tsvetkov V.Y. Spatial knowledge: Formation and representation., Saarbrucken, 2013. -107 c.

340. Davis D. R., Dingel J. I. A spatial knowledge economy //American Economic Review. - 2019. - T. 109. - №. 1. - C. 153-170.

341. Gohar A., Nencioni G. The role of 5G technologies in a smart city: The case for intelligent transport system //Sustainability. - 2021. - T. 13. - №. 9. - C.

5188.

342. Tsvetkov V.Y., Rosenberg I.N. Intelligent transport systems - Saarbrucken, 2012. - 297 c.

343. Kovalenko N.I. Knowledge extraction for intellectuals transport systems // Perspectives of science and education - 2014. - №5. - c.4552.

344. Gohar A., Nencioni G. The role of 5G technologies in a smart city: The case for intelligent transport system //Sustainability. - 2021. - T. 13. - №. 9. - C. 5188.

345. Tsvetkov V.Ya. Management with the use of cyber-physical systems // Perspectives of Science and Education. - 2017. - №3(27). - c.55-60

346. Zanero S. Cyber-physical systems //Computer. - 2017. - T. 50. - №. 4. - C. 14-16.

347. Levin B.A., Tsvetkov V.Ya. Cyberphysical systems in transport management // Transport World. - 2018. T. 16. № 2 (75). - C. 138-145

348. Alguliyev R., Imamverdiyev Y., Sukhostat L. Cyber-physical systems and their security issues //Computers in Industry. - 2018. - T. 100. - C. 212-223.

349. Levin B.A., Tsvetkov V.Ya. Digital railway: principles and technologies // World of Transport. - 2018. - T. 16. - №3 (76). - c. 50-61.

350. V. Ya. Tsvetkov, S.V. Shaytura, K.V. Ordov. Digital management railway // Advances in Economics, Business and Management Research, volume 105. 1st International Scientific and Practical Conference on Digital Economy (ISCDE 2019), p. 181- 185.

351. Tsvetkov V.Ya. Spatial relations in geoinformatics// Earth Sciences. - 2012. - №1. - c.59-61

352. Yip K., Zhao F. Spatial aggregation: theory and applications //Journal of Artificial Intelligence Research. - 1996. - T. 5. - C. 1-26.

353. Bailey-Kellogg C., Zhao F. Qualitative spatial reasoning extracting and reasoning with spatial aggregates //AI Magazine. - 2003. - T. 24. - №. 4. - C. 47-47.

354. Del Bimbo A., Vicario E., Zingoni D. A spatial logic for symbolic description of image contents // Journal of Visual Languages & Computing. - 1994. - V.5. - №. 3. - C. 267-286

355. Kravets E. A. Cartographic logic (analysis of the issues of the state and environmental protection): monograph - M.: Izd-vo MIIGAiK, 2010.160c

356. Lyutiy A.A. Map language: essence, system, functions. - 2nd ed. - M.: GEOS, 2002. - 327 c/

357. Bertrand Russell. Vagueness. In John Slater, editor (1923) , *Essays on Language, Mind, and Matter 1919-26,* The Collected Papers of Bertrand

Russell, pages 145 - 154. Unwin Hyman, London/

358. Kontchakov R. et al. Spatial logic+ temporal logic=? //Handbook of spatial logics. - Springer, Dordrecht, 2007. - C. 497-564.

359. Tarski, Alfred (1956). Foundations of the geometry of solids. In *Logic, Semantics, and Metamathematics*, pages 24-29. Clarendon Press, Oxford

360. Markelov B.M. Spatial information as a factor of management // State Counsellor. - 2013. - №4. - c34-38.

361. Savinykh V.P., Tsvetkov V.Ya. Geodata as systemic information resource // Bulletin of the Russian Academy of Sciences, 2014, Vol. 84, No. 9, pp. 826-829.

362. Ozherel'eva T.A. System analysis of spatial innovation // Ozherel'eva T.A. System analysis of spatial innovation // International Journal of Applied and Fundamental Research. - 2013, - №12 - c.116-120.

363. Tsvetkov V. Ya. Informatisation, innovation processes and geoinformation technologies // Izvestiya vysokikh uchebnykh obrazovaniye. Geodesy and aerial photography - 2006. - №4. - c.112-118

364. Tsvetkov V. Y., Omelchenko A.. S. Innovation and innovative process as a complex system // Quality, Innovations, Education. - 2006. - №2. - c.11- 14

365. Rosenberg I.N., Soloviev I.V., Tsvetkov V.Ya. Complex innovations in the management of complex organisational and technical systems. / edited by V.I. Yakunin - M.: Feoria, 2010 - 248 p.

366. Matchin V.T. Updating of databases with spatial data information // Slavic Forum, 2015. - 3(9) - c.173-180

367. Tsvetkov V.Ya. Updates of spatial information // Educational Resources and Technology. - 2015. - №3 (11). - c.110 -116/

368. V. Ya. Tsvetkov. Spatial Relations Economy // European Journal of Economic Studies, 2013, No. 1(3). - p.57-60

369. Lototsky V.L. Spatial information modelling // Educational resources and technologies. - 2016. - 3 (15). - c.114-122.

370. Gospodinov, S.G. Digital spatial modelling (in Russian) // Earth Sciences. - 2019. - №3. - c.4-15.

371. Bolbakov R. G. G. G., Popov K. S. High-performance processing of spatial information of large volumes and flows // Educational Resources and Technologies - 2020. - № 3 (32). - C. 80-88.

372. Buravtsev A.V., Tsvetkov V.Ya. Cloud computing for big geospatial data // Information and Space. 2019. - №3. -c .110-115

373. Levin B.A., Tsvetkov V.Ya. Information processes in the space of "big

data" // World of Transport. 2017. - T.15, №6(73). - c.20-30.

374.    Tsvetkov V. Ya. Integer Coordinates as an Nanotechnological
Instrument // Nanotechnology Research and Practice. - 2014, 4(4), pp. 230-236.

375.    Chekharin E.E. Algorithms for interpretation of remote sensing data
probing. // Slavic Forum, 2015. - 3(9) - c.301-308.

376.    Ryabtseva N. K., Kotov R. G. Information processes and machine
learning. G. Information processes and machine
translation: linguistic aspect. - Nauka, 1986.

377.    Tsvetkov V. Ya. The Cognitive Modeling with the Use of Spatial
Information // European Journal of Technology and Design. - 2015, 4 (10), pp.
149158.

378.    Kipyatkova I. S., Karpov A. A. Automatic processing and
statistical analysis of news text corpus for the language model of Russian speech
recognition system //Information and control systems. - 2010. - №. 4.

379.    Artstein R., Poesio M. Inter-coder agreement for computational linguistics
//Computational Linguistics. - 2008. - V. 34. - №. 4. - p.555-596

380.    Ermakov A.E., Pleshko V.V. Semantic interpretation in
systems of computer text analysis // Information technologies. - 2009. - N 6. - C.
2-7.

381.    Tsvetkov V.Ya. Solution of reverse photogrammetric serif under
additional conditions// Izvestiya vysshee obrazovaniya vysshee obrazovaniya
[Izvestia of Higher Educational Institutions]. Geodesy and aerial photography.
1998- №2 c. 94-98.

382.    Dyshlenko, S.G. Direct and inverse spatial problem (in Russian) //
Slavic Forum. - 2017. - 1(15). - c.210-217

383.    Dyshlenko S.G. Spatial problems - Saarbruken, 2019. -110
c.

384.    Tsvetkov V. Ya. The Problem of Asteroid-Comet Danger // Russian
Journal of Astrophysical Research. Series A. 2016, 1 (2), pp. 33-40/

385.    Titov E.K.. Algorithms of situational information processing // Slavic
Forum. -2018. - 4 (22). - c.60-64.

386.    Titov E.K. Methods and algorithms of situational calculations -
Saarbruken, 2020. -225c/

387.    Tsvetkov V.Ya., Titov E.K. Information Computing
situation // Slavic Forum. -2019. - 4(26). - c.389-397.

388.    Oznamets V.V. Processing of images from BILA using projective
algorithms // Earth Sciences. - 2019. - №3. - c. 16-25.

389.    Efimov A. I. et al. Image processing in multispectral
vision systems // Vestnik of Ryazan State Radio-Technical University. - 2017. -

№. 60. - C. 83.

390.   Prokhorenok N. A. OpenCV and Java. Image processing and Computer vision. - BHV-Peterburg, 2018.

391.   Tomakova R. A., Petrik E. A. Methods and algorithms of digitalisation image processing. - 2020/

Printed by Books on Demand GmbH, Norderstedt / Germany